SO YO

Born in Manchester in
home, Roy Trevivian
then served in the RA
After that he scraped
sports than at examina

In 1947 he was ordained
churches on the Liverpool Docks and in the Old Kent Road. Eight years later he was ordained an Anglican priest, becoming curate of a housing estate on the Epsom Downs and then vicar of another housing estate in Guildford. From 1964 to 1973 he was a full-time radio producer with the BBC. Since 1975 he has been chaplain to the Mayflower Centre in the East End of London.

Mr Trevivian writes out of his own difficult experience, which includes three periods in mental hospital. A Christian for forty years, he says he has remained so at times 'only by the skin of my teeth', but is more convinced than ever about the basic truth of the Christian faith.

by the same author

WHAT THEY BELIEVE

ROY TREVIVIAN

SO YOU'RE LONELY

COLLINS
Fount Paperbacks

First published by Fount Paperbacks 1978
Second Impression October 1980

Made and printed in Great Britain by
William Collins Sons & Co Ltd, Glasgow

With love
to Yvonne, Carolyn and David

Acknowledgements

To be brought up in a Christian home is a great advantage, even though at the time it meant very little. But at least I learned from my parents that it was possible that the Christian faith might be true.

Thanks to Joyce Crane and Frances Chalk who typed their heads off for me.

Thanks to Chris Barrow who worked hard with the grammar, spelling and punctuation, which are mainly mysteries to me.

Thanks to Myrtle Powley who was the first person to realize that I might have this book inside me and encouraged me to get it out.

Thanks to two psychiatrists at the London Hospital who are the new breed of that profession, who do not believe that the answers to life's problems lie in drugs but in relationships.

Thanks to the countless people whose paths have crossed mine who have been honest, open, loving and trusting, and to those who have brought their problems to me and from whom I have learned so much. And to those whose patience I have tried to the utmost but who have gone on caring for me.

Thanks to the people in Canning Town who accepted me when I had almost nothing to give to them.

My deepest thanks to the three people to whom this book is dedicated, my wife and children, from whom I have learned more than I could ever express about what true relationship is all about.

Acknowledgements continued

And just as deep, my thanks to the living Jesus who had he not still been alive, I wouldn't have been.

And to those who having read this book have found that it has helped, you will have made my journey worthwhile; and those who having read it consider that what I have said is a load of old rubbish, well, you might be right, but on the other hand I have the temerity to wonder if you are! O.K.?

And to Lady Collins, Lesley Walmsley and David Edwards who got this book published. What faith they must have!

And to Malcolm Muggeridge for so much.

Roy Trevivian

Mayflower Centre,
London E.16,
June 1978.

Contents

Introduction

Anyone who has worked with Roy Trevivian, or had occasion to observe him at work during his years with the Religious Broadcasting Department of the BBC, cannot but have recognized his unusual flair and talent. Take him for all in all, I should rate him as the most effective professional broadcaster I ever encountered in this particular field – itself a curious no-man's-land lying between show business and evangelism. His very weaknesses and amiabilities enhanced his appeal; his pieties were too human to offend, and too real to bear the taint of clerical expertise. Indeed, it was difficult to see him as a clergyman at all, and once, when I happened to come upon him in full parsonical rig, I could scarcely believe it was the Roy Trevivian I knew. Spiritually, he surely belongs to a pre-Anglican era. I find it easy to imagine him roaming about the highways of Europe in the brown habit of an early Franciscan, or for that matter among the stragglers who followed Jesus around. But a beneficed vicar – no!

My own first acquaintance with him was as an interviewer. He arrived with a tape-recorder and began to ask questions. This is a business full of pitfalls. There is the interviewer who comes with prepared questions and goes doggedly through them. Responding is such a case is like filling in one of those interminable forms the Inland Revenue or Immigration authorities so delight in devising. Then there is the interviewer who takes one through one's *curriculum vitae*, hastily and usually inaccurately culled from *Who's Who* or some other work of reference. Or the one who relies on an amiable chat, but invariably gets the names of one's books wrong, and is even liable to imagine one is someone else. Not to mention the attractive young woman who, visibly awed, browses through voluminous notes in longhand and fumbles with her tape-recorder, only to find after a long conversation that she has pressed the wrong button and recorded nothing.

It goes without saying that Roy laboured under none of these disabilities. He asked me about the things he really wanted to know, and what he wanted to know seemed precisely what I wanted to tell him. From the beginning a warm and harmonious atmosphere was created; more than anything else, it is this warmth and good nature in Roy's disposition which makes him so effective a broadcaster. Unlike other forms of communication – writing, for instance – broadcasting requires pre-eminently to generate a sense of nearness, not just to the particular individual the broadcaster happens to be talking with or interviewing, but also to unseen listeners or viewers. Though absent, they are present; each and every one of them. The demagogue requires his audience's actual physical presence to function effectively, whereas the broadcaster is under the necessity of addressing his audience *in absentia*, as it were – which is why some brilliant orators like Aneurin Bevan, and Churchill when he had no script to read, make poor broadcasters. An image himself, the broadcaster must relate to other images; he is a shadow addressing shadows. This trafficking in images is a great strain under which numerous practitioners, from Gilbert Harding onwards, have cracked. I feel sure it had more to do with Roy's crackup when it came than he is perhaps even now aware.

His interview with me proceeded easily and pleasurably. Roy is the easiest person in the world to talk with about religion. Whatever doubts may assail him, and misfortunes afflict him, he remains an enthusiast for Jesus, about whom he always speaks as though he were some dear and wonderful friend and companion whom he has lately left. I find this very beautiful. In the truest sense of the word he is an essentially religious man – actually, something of a rarity in religious broadcasting set-ups, including the BBC's. By this I mean that one senses an awareness in him that at the very heart of our earthly existence there lies a mystery, not a proposition; that the exploration of this mystery is the supreme purpose of living at all, and can only be undertaken through the imagination rather than the mind, in terms of love rather than power, and under the aegis of the Incarnation rather than of any scholastic, scientific or other mundane discipline. I do not say that Roy would put it in these words, or even that he would necessarily approve of them as words, but from the beginning I detected, as I thought, such an awareness in him, expressed most cogently in his companionship with Jesus and love for him, and in the glow this gave to his own inner life and relations with his fellow humans. When the darkness gathered and descended upon him, the glow diminished, almost to the point of extinction, but never quite went out; so that when the darkness lifted, as it did, the glow was still there, ready to burgeon again. This is the story of his crackup, which he tells very simply, movingly and honestly in *So You're Lonely*.

After our interview I saw Roy from time to time. He visited us again in Robertsbridge, this time with his wife and children, and we met occasionally in the studios. He was doing a lot of broadcasting one way and another, always competently, and sometimes outstandingly. One of his programmes – *Speakeasy* – was a notable success. It was when I went on this programme, and saw him after a long interval, that I realized how great a strain he was under. However, everything seemed to be going well with him, and he might reasonably have expected to stay on with the BBC, increasing in importance and salary as the years passed, and retiring ultimately on a sufficient pension. In the event, this did not happen; he left the BBC with the usual farewells and festivities, and we who admired and were fond of him wondered from time to time how he was faring, and whether anything could be done to give him a helping hand. In such cases one easily falls into the role of a remote and ineffectual Samaritan.

As he recounts without self-pity, or any kind of breast-beating, like Céline he went to the end of the night, except that, for him, the night ended in a dawn breaking; his friend Jesus saw him through. It was a Scott-Fitzgerald-type crackup, in which alcohol and psychiatric wards played their sinister parts. For Roy the supreme horror was the loneliness – his own and of so many around him. Broadcasting is a gregarious occupation, and he had grown used to being always with people; now he was alone, unwanted, rejected as he thought. His book is about loneliness, which in our time is the lot of so many, especially the afflicted. With all the talk of caring and concern, all the institutions of welfare and counselling, all the cadres of social workers, in the high-rise buildings so many sit alone, as along the thronging streets so many walk alone.

Roy writes of this omnipresent loneliness from his own personal experience; of how the various ostensible antidotes – alcohol, sex, drugs – only serve in the end to intensify it; of how even the family can easily prove too fragile a breakwater when the great waves of loneliness come rolling in. Likewise he recalls some of his own bitterest moments; as when, stretched out on a bed in the dark in a mental hospital, he was visited by the devil, or at any rate heard a voice insisting that there was no love in the world, only appetites; no hope, only the exigencies of time and the urgencies of the flesh; no destiny beyond the ticking of the clocks. Even then he remembered that the loneliest man ever, nailed to a cross, heard a similar voice telling him that God had abandoned him and that his sacrifice was in vain. Yet from this same man in his desperate plight had come the most audacious hopes, the most sublime love and joy, ever to be entertained by the human heart. It was this thought alone that enabled Roy to get up from his bed, face the world again, as he has, and write his book for the comfort of others.

In it he offers no panacea, no packaged pick-me-up or bank-me-down; only the story of his own dark night of the soul, and how he emerged from it more confident than ever that the good news proclaimed in the gospels remains valid, and that he who first proclaimed the good news, as he promised, remains among us, and accessible to all who seek comfort and help. I found it an uplifting, heartening and absorbing story, as, I trust, will many others.

Malcolm Muggeridge

Robertsbridge
June 1978

Chapter 1

Is This Your Problem?

Only yesterday I talked with a Christian man who gave the appearance of great success. Extrovert, energetic, an organizer, a beaming smile. But it was his eyes that gave the game away. Only 28, but married to a woman who suffered from chronic depression and anxiety that became total panic. At the end of his day's work he went home with dread. He doesn't blame her for her condition. But the burden of caring for her, having to take her violent explosions of despair and hate for life, God and other people, compared with periods when she withdraws totally within herself, is destroying him. Until yesterday he carried all this alone amongst people who thought he hadn't a care in the world.

It was midnight. It was March. It was twelve years ago. I was standing alongside a car at the Marble Arch in London, because the car had broken down. I was on my way to a cellar in Soho where I knew that a concert of folk singing was taking place between midnight and the early hours of the morning.

In those days I was producing programmes for the BBC, and I was looking for folk singers with talent who had something worthwhile to say through their songs. It was midnight, the car wouldn't go, and it was belting down with rain. I was fed up to the teeth and I wanted to go home. But I didn't, and I'm glad I didn't. It was two hours later that I arrived at the folk club after a visit from the Automobile Association's breakdown van. The club was packed. I just managed to find a place for my bottom on the concrete floor. I listened to several singers, all rather feeble. And then it happened. A young man climbed on to the tiny stage and began to sing. The atmosphere became electric. He held the people in that packed club in the palm of his hand. When he had finished I edged over to where he had gone. He was sitting in a corner of the room. I asked him for his name. He said he was Paul Simon. The name meant nothing. What was he doing in England? He was a law student over here from the United States on a student's visa. Was he allowed to work for money? No. Would he record some songs for the BBC if I arranged a work permit? Yes, he would be delighted to do that.

Thus it was that for the first time the people in Britain heard Paul Simon over the air, Paul Simon who today is known by millions. I paid him £25 for one hour's work. In that one hour he recorded twelve songs. I remember them all, but three more especially.

Those three are 'I am a Rock', 'The Sound of Silence', and 'He was my Brother'. They all spoke of loneliness, isolation and alienation. And they spoke movingly and profoundly.

'I am a Rock' told of the way we all separate ourselves from each other because we are afraid of getting hurt if through loving someone we get close to them. 'The Sound of Silence' told of how we speak to each other but never say anything, and of how we listen to each other without hearing what is actually said. 'He was my Brother' is about a friend of Paul's who was black and when taking part in a freedom ride in the United States was shot dead, and the song is a cry of pain about the way we alienate whole groups of people who are not of our class, colour or creed.

Those songs, particularly the first two, are now world famous and have sold by the million on discs. I have never forgotten them, nor the passion with which Paul sang them in that basement studio in Broadcasting House in London.

It is so true that we all hide from each other. There are parts of me that I wouldn't want you to see. There are parts of you that you keep hidden from even your closest friend. We are afraid to love, because love makes us vulnerable and makes demands. So we talk mostly in trivialities, the communication is very much on the surface, the silence between us is immense. And here we are, each locked in the prison of our own ego, afraid to come out, driven to all kinds of behaviour in order to keep our defences intact. I look into people's eyes and behind the mask that they are wearing I can see the hunger in their souls for acceptance, understanding, and love for who they really are.

We live in a world filled with very lonely people, each of us desperate to love and be loved, to feel the warmth and closeness of another human being, but the panic we would feel if we came out from behind our barred and locked up cells is so great that we choose to live with the desperation of loneliness instead.

A widow of 42 told me recently that since her husband died three years ago she has only been half alive. Her life had revolved around him. See her at a party and she joins in with gusto. Sit with her at home alone and she is empty, dead.

I know many men who are living apart from their wives and families. Some because they have been violent and the wife has been to court to get an injunction to prohibit him from entering the matrimonial home. Others because of drink, are similarly barred from their home. They come to me, often in tears, full of repentance, saying, 'If only she would have me back, I can't go on living without her', and with suicide in their minds.

In dockland where I live, men in their late forties and early fifties are becoming redundant because the docks are rapidly closing down. Likewise, other large employers are cutting down on their work force. A man last week sat alone at home fairly drunk. The threat of redundancy had hung over him for two years. That threat had driven him to drink. Now redundancy had happened. He was out of work at 51. What do you do when for 36 years you have been a docker? Your identity as a human being has been invested in your role as a docker and then you are no longer one. Whoever you have been has now gone; who are you now? A crisis of personal identity may occur, and drink, mental breakdown and thoughts of suicide can follow very quickly. There are 1,500,000 people in Britain out of work and the politicians say it may get worse. Just think of the terribly destructive effect those people are facing. When you are out of work for whatever reason, you are outside society, you don't belong, you have no role, no identity, you are lost. Many turn to petty crime and if they are put in prison, then prison will complete the job of destroying them as responsible human beings. You become a number. There is no 'you' to make decisions, what 'you' there is left gets buried.

When I worked for the BBC I produced a programme about agoraphobia. This is a condition that can hit anyone, but mostly women. The symptom is a complete inability to go out of doors alone, and in severe cases such people can't go out at all. They stay indoors and in every way give the appearance of being perfectly normal. Their families can't understand them. 'Don't be silly', they are told. But to cross their front doorstep into the street paralyses them with terror. After the programme we got masses of letters from people who thought that they and they alone were the only ones in this condition. Letters from husbands who at last began to understand their wives. A woman called Alice Neville, who had been a sufferer, started an organization called 'The Open Door' to help such people and she now knows of thousands with this problem.

Loneliness. It comes in many forms. The homosexual or lesbian who daren't reveal the truth. Women who were never invited to marry. Widows, widowers. The mentally sick. People living alone in high-rise flats. The elderly. Loneliness and the feeling of rejection and alienation are becoming increasingly common.

It is sometimes called 'The English Disease'. Little English boys are taught that it isn't manly to cry. We talk of 'keeping a stiff upper lip'. Don't 'wear your heart on your sleeve': we mustn't touch each other. I know people who are terrified of touching or being touched. None of us like the 'moaner' and particularly the person who seems to 'enjoy' his misery. But there are masses of people who wear a brave face to hide a lonely, breaking heart. It is to you that I want to speak, because I have walked that road and know what that road is like.

When I was the chaplain of a mental hospital I met this condition in its most acute form. In those days it was called schizophrenia, or at least it was one of the forms that the disease took. I sat with people who otherwise sat on their own. They never spoke. They looked with unseeing eyes into a void. Some sat completely motionless. Some sat and just picked at their clothing. They couldn't communicate with me, nor I with them. To observe them you would have thought they were the 'living dead'. But the psychiatrist told me that within the sometimes motionless body there was a mind that was ablaze with activity, but the activity consisted only of fantasies. They had retreated completely within their own private world and that world had no connection with reality.

Where had 'they' gone? Was there a person within that shell? Had there ever been a person there? My answer was and is, yes. But because they were afraid of the outside world, the world outside their 'self', they had erected huge barriers between themselves and the world. They had been hurt by the world too much; they had had enough and they were 'gone'. What sort of world is it that can do that to people? Whether you like it or not, this world is that kind of world. We call this sort of person insane. But it is my view that we are all insane to a greater or lesser degree. All of us retreat from reality at some points. All of us find the world too threatening in some areas. Everyone who reads this book, if you are honest, knows what I mean.

I do not come to you as a knight in shining armour to rescue the damsel in distress. My own history includes three periods in mental hospital as a patient. It includes being broken, lost and terrified. But I am still alive and I have made some discoveries and if, my frightened friend, you can stretch out your hand and hold mine, maybe what I have discovered may help you. That is the only reason this book is being written.

CHAPTER 2

One Cause of Loneliness

It is my conviction that God never intended anyone to be lonely. Whether you believe that the story of Adam is historically true or not, that story enshrines a truth about the human condition. No person is born to live in isolation. That was never God's plan. The Book of Genesis says that God said it wasn't good for Adam to live without a companion, so God gave Adam a companion called Eve. She was a woman and speaking from what Hebrew I learnt 30 years ago the word 'woman' means someone else – it means 'someone who was separate from Adam but who would be his friend'.

Loneliness is against God's will. That doesn't mean that if you are lonely you are necessarily evil. It could mean that, but not necessarily so. Loneliness is bad, evil and destructive and it must be banished. But what causes it?

There are many causes.

Start with a simple one. A man I know was a Japanese prisoner of war. He worked on the Burma Railway. He saw hundreds of his comrades die from starvation, overwork or brutality. He survived – just. Broken in body and mind he is still alive, living in a one-bedroomed flat (did I say living?) in a tower block in Canning Town in East London. He only goes out to get his shopping. As far as I know, apart from people here at the Mayflower, no one calls on him regularly. Who were the unimaginative clowns who planned tower blocks and put him in one? Tower blocks are of the devil. I know lots of people who live in them and although their close proximity to one another should encourage people to be more friendly, the very opposite happens. On a typical landing there are five flats, and yet over and over again the people who live there tell me that not only do they not meet their neighbours but they take great precautions not to meet them. In the area where I live there used to be old, slum streets where people used to know each other. Hitler and the post-war bull-dozers destroyed those streets. People used to sit in their front doorways and smile at or talk with neighbours as they passed by. My great-auntie Nancy lived in such a street in Bolton in Lancashire. She always wore clogs. She was the 'layer out' for the street whenever a death occurred. Everyone knew Auntie Nancy and she knew them – and everyone knew each other.

But in the name of 'progress' the streets have gone and in their place we have these ghastly, clinical high-rise blocks designed by men who live in lovely houses with private swimming pools in the heart of Kent, Essex, Surrey and Sussex. May God have mercy on their souls and the men and women in authority who commissioned these high-rise flats.

Our local mental hospital did a statistical study of what happened to people who live in high-rise blocks and they found that above a certain height the incidence of mental breakdown galloped. Is anyone in authority prepared to demolish these monstrosities and house people properly or are there other considerations more important than people?

From 1949 to 1953 I lived and worked on the Old Kent Road. In four years I never met a single person with a serious mental illness and I never heard of one broken marriage. Since then 'they' have ruined the Old Kent Road with 'progress' and if Canning Town, where I live now, is anything to go by (it is, because the Old Kent Road and Canning Town used to be very similar communities and they have both been 'improved'), then the Old Kent Road is in the mess we are in here in Canning Town. Broken marriages all over the place, bucketfuls of tranquillizers, anti-depressants and sleeping pills. None of which work. Why? Because the old togetherness, the feeling that you belonged, the knowledge that in 'the street' you had friends, the security of knowing that if you were in trouble, sickness, unemployment, death, 'the street' wouldn't let you down – all that has gone. There are no 'streets' now in Canning Town – just 'progress' – which means that instead of preserving communities 'they' at this very moment are making deserts of the streets that breathed warmth and security, and in their place 'they' will build the most hideous 'units of accommodation' that look just like prison blocks.

What *are* we doing?

The trouble is, of course, that the people who 'plan' these horrors don't have to live in them. The Prime Minister has No. 10 Downing Street, 'Chequers' a country mansion, and his own private house. What sort of accommodation does the Minister of the Environment have? Where does the Minister of Housing live? To say nothing of the Minister of Health?

Jesus had nowhere to lay his head.

The King of Kings! Then you think of Buckingham Palace, Sandringham, Balmoral and the Royal Yacht *Britannia*. Rule Britannia! Who was ruling when the tower block called Ronan Point (ten minutes' walk from where I am writing this) fell down?

In the late 1950s I was the vicar of a parish in Guildford where the borough was building a huge new council estate. I knocked on hundreds of doors – except that the doors didn't have knockers, I had to rattle the letter-boxes. Every letter-box was identical. 'Was there a way,' I wondered, 'to give each house individuality and therefore help the occupants to feel like individuals and not just part of a congested whole?' Yes, there was a way. If only each home could have its own front garden. One family would grow hollyhocks, another roses, another hydrangeas. What they had, in fact, was one long length of grass stretching in front of every house and the occupants of the houses weren't allowed to cultivate it and make it individual.

I protested and said that each family should have their own front garden to cultivate in their own individual way. The Chairman of the Housing Committee fought me bitterly and he won. But I did go to see his house and it was surrounded by gardens and lawns, with the whole thing enclosed with a high, tree-lined fence! What was good for him was too good for his clients.

Human beings are very odd. We need to be individuals and to be able to express it before we can relate to each other. In the old days, the East End of London produced 'characters' – individuals, even though they lived in slums. The 'planners' have abolished the slums and with it individuals, so that people are losing their sense of identity and with that there is no relating, as each person withdraws into a mental, inward void and the community as a community dies. I am not advocating slums. God forbid! But I am totally opposed to a housing policy that destroys the personal identity of individuals and hence makes living, vibrant, community life impossible. If you are the same as me, what is the point of us meeting? But if you are different then we are both enriched by the meeting, provided we are both prepared to accept that we are both unique individuals. *Vive la différence!*

You may think that where and how people live doesn't matter. But it does. Jesus could live anywhere. In his later life he didn't have a home – but his environment affected him. If not, why did he escape from the crowds to retreat into the hills? During his last weeks on earth he spent the days with the teeming masses in Jerusalem, but at night he retired to the tiny village of Bethany to relax with his friends, Mary, Martha and Lazarus.

If he needed to be alone or with friends, don't we? In London and Birmingham and Liverpool, etc., you can be lonely but never alone. In those places it is becoming more and more difficult even to have friends.

I spend very little of my time in pubs. But the few I have been in have a juke box playing so loudly that it is impossible to have a conversation. My own daughter told me that at a disco if you can hear what another person is saying to you then the 'group' shouldn't be employed. I am beginning to understand what Mick Jagger and the Rolling Stones are all about. Stop me thinking. Stop me talking. Stop me listening to people. Stop me relating. Create loneliness – that is what tower blocks and some pop groups are saying.

And in the meantime, the mental hospitals fill to overflowing. Drugs and alcohol flow in torrents. Violence bred from anger and frustration cascades around us. And we wonder why.

Even when the slave trade was at its height, was there ever a time when the worth of the individual was considered to be as little as it is now?

We talk of the unemployed and forget that each one has a name. We talk about the Working Class and the Middle Class and the Upper Class, and forget that each one has a name – Fred, Adrian or Lord Alfred.

Elderly people don't have names, they are OAPs (Old Age Pensioners) or Senior Citizens.

Men and women in prison aren't people, they are 'the prison population'.

'Juvenile delinquents' aren't Bill, Fred and Janet, they are 'undisciplined kids'.

Even the Civil Service aren't people, each with his own personal joys and pains, they are 'faceless' bureaucrats.

Please God, save us from collective nouns and let us deal in personal names, even personal pronouns!

In the Garden of the Resurrection, Jesus said, 'Mary', and she knew what he meant. And when he said that she knew who was speaking to her.

CHAPTER 3

Loneliness: Sex and Marriage

I am 56. I am male. I am heterosexual. I have some friends who are homosexual or lesbian, or 'gay' as they prefer to be called. But we all have a common problem. The one sex doesn't understand the other. I don't care what my 'gay' friends say, if they are biologically male or female they don't understand how the other half feel or think, and nor do the rest of us.

Professor Bronowski in his *Ascent of Man* argued that originally there wasn't male and female as separate people. Both sexes existed in the one person. Atheist though he was, he corroborated the Book of Genesis. Originally there was one person and out of that one person there emerged Adam and Eve as man and woman.

So here we are, male and female. Jesus said that in heaven that would be done away with, but for the time being we are stuck with the difference. For a long time in our civilization we emphasized the difference by treating females as inferior to males. Now we have 'Women's Lib'. The only trouble that I can see is that women want to become men and men want to become women.

So we are split, but want to heal the rift. Jesus said that we should become one flesh. But we won't achieve it by women becoming more like men or men becoming more like women.

We shall only achieve this by men understanding women and women understanding men. Changing our outward appearances is only a 'cop-out'. The loneliest experience that exists is when a woman loves a man and doesn't understand what makes him 'tick', and the other way round.

I really do know something about all this. I get frustrated by married men who claim that their wives don't understand them, or married women who charge their husbands with the same offence. It doesn't seem to occur to them that what they should be engaged in is understanding their partner, instead of waiting for the opposite to happen.

It's all right before you get married. If the going gets rough you can always opt out. But if you have said those mind-boggling words 'For better or for worse, forsaking all other, in sickness and in health, I will stand by you till I die', do people realize what they are taking on?

One party who hasn't got the foggiest idea what makes the other party 'tick', pledges to forsake all others till they die, and then realizes that they are stuck with a total mystery, i.e. their partner.

So marriages break down. Some people don't get divorced but the partners go on drifting further and further away from each other. I know many marriages where the partners don't communicate in any real way, but for the sake of appearances stay together.

Physical sex draws people together and for a little while the physical pleasure gives them the illusion that they are close. But then the truth that they are not close as people begins to be acknowledged, and sex either becomes just animal or ceases to happen. But they still live together, each in their own loneliness. When there are children they feel that they must stay together and often they do, living a completely lonely life. Or else they have 'affairs', each keeping what they are doing secret from the other. What a ghastly way to live. This situation causes the partners to hate each other. Some try to hide the hate, but the children know it is there. Often the hate explodes into physical violence, with the expected results on the children.

I have never met the perfect marriage. I have known some where the joy outweighed the sorrow. I have known others where the 'working arrangement' has succeeded. Others where they have stayed together in hell. Others where they have separated but with one partner still longing for the other, and others where the separation has been complete and each made a new life. But even then, except in a few rare instances, they have married again and made exactly the same mistakes.

So why don't we own up and face the terrible fact that very few of us are capable of a true, full, life-enhancing relationship with someone of the opposite sex? No wonder that some people become monks and others nuns, and that the Roman Catholic priesthood is celibate.

To create babies men and women have to come together. By far the best environment for a newborn child is the full, free, loving relationship between father and mother. Theology and the Bible say that we are all fallen, so that no matter who we are, we have been damaged by our parents and we in turn will damage our children and so the dreadful treadmill keeps turning. Is there no way of breaking this vicious circle?

The vast majority of adults in Britain are married. I ask myself how many of them are lonely. They will try to persuade me and themselves that they are not. But they know, and they know that I know, that they are.

In his loneliness a teenaged boy finds a girl. He falls in love. He explores her body and derives pleasure in doing so. Does he explore who she is? Does she explore who he is? For that is what it is all about.

Physical, sexual exploration is only another way of saying, 'I'm lonely, you could ease the pain I feel'. The trouble is that sexual satisfaction doesn't in itself cancel out the loneliness.

Some of the loneliest people in the world are prostitutes and the men who go to them. No one with any compassion will condemn them, but we must condemn a culture that has encouraged them to believe that physical sex alone will help them to feel less lonely. Miss Buckingham, a prostitute, 'does not allow her clients to talk about themselves' – *Guardian* newspaper, 10 August 1977.

In a way, physical sexuality is an attempt to make a person whole. It never works. But we all have this feeling that it should work. Why do you think that Jesus said that in heaven there is neither male nor female, there is neither marriage nor giving in marriage? Why did he say that? Loneliness is not ended by sexual experience or marriage. There must be another way, but saying that will not stop anyone from trying it out, because we have all been conditioned to believe that 'falling in love' and having someone fall in love with us will mean the end of our loneliness. It does not.

It is, of course, completely wrong to generalize about marriage on the basis of marriages one has known. But in my role as a clergyman and as a counsellor, and as a married man, I have had a lot of dealings with marriage.

There are husbands who want sex with a wife who has lost all interest in it. There are husbands who, as the years go by, find their wives less and less attractive, spending more and more of their time outside the home, either with their men friends or some other woman. The man goes out to try to answer his problem of loneliness. The woman stays at home to face hers. And the reverse can and does happen, with the woman seeking attention and sexual fulfilment with another man.

It seems to me a fact that some men marry a woman who represents for them a substitute mother. Sometimes this works without too much tension. But how lonely a woman must feel who, instead of having a mate, has to live with a little boy. And how lonely for a man who wants a grown-up woman as a mate, only to find that what he has got is a little girl.

I was helping a couple recently where the woman had married a father substitute. Sex between her and her husband was emotionally painful for her, and after it she was overwhelmed with guilt. Why? Because planted within all of us is a deep fear of incest, and to commit incest can create the most terrible feelings of guilt. The Church has always disapproved of marriage between blood relations. For reasons that I don't understand, a child born of a liaison between blood relations can often result in the child being damaged physically or mentally. The Church is being utterly sensible in refusing to marry blood relations. Eventually the woman I have in mind couldn't sleep with her husband and finally couldn't share the same bedroom with him. The guilt of possible incest was very powerful.

Night after night he slept alone in the spare bedroom, and yet day after day he was with a woman he longed for and was married to but wasn't allowed to touch. Being a Christian, he didn't seek relief with some other woman, but the loneliness, the feelings of not being wanted, sapped all his self-confidence, brought on depression and drove him to the psychiatrist. It was no easier for her because although she didn't know why she didn't want him, she did not realize the pain it was causing him. And her guilt, when she found out, was almost unbearable. Blaming either party would get nowhere. They were trapped within the darkness of loneliness and through no fault of their own.

The little boy in the husband needs a mother or the little girl in the wife needs a father. The little-boy-husband becomes suffocatingly dependent on the mother-wife or the little-girl-wife becomes equally dependent on the father-husband. This dependency gives rise to a most destructive possessiveness and the jealousies it arouses can become murderous. 'I need you so much,' the little child cries, 'you mustn't give anything of yourself to anyone else, you are mine, mine, MINE.'

A parasite that lives off a tree can eventually destroy the tree, and then the parasite dies because the tree is dead. It's the same with a marriage where the partners go on living together and one partner is living off the other, and they become strangers simply existing under the same roof. You can see these people in any pub, any café, just sitting together, neither of them speaking, no communication between them. A few inches away physically but as people a million miles apart.

We all need something of a parent in our mate from time to time, because all of us have something of the child still within us. At times the husband has to be strong when his wife needs support, and the wife has to be strong when the husband needs understanding. That seems to me to be quite normal. What bothers me is when the wife has to be mother most of the time or the husband has to be father. Therein lies terrible loneliness for the one who has to be parent. Loneliness for the one being the child only strikes home when the one who is playing the child role loses their partner through desertion, unfaithfulness or death.

God gave Eve to Adam, not to be his mother nor his child, but to be someone who could stand alone in her own right and be a companion on equal terms, to be what we ought to mean when we call a husband or wife a mate.

But what about people who don't get married? There are some who quite rationally prefer the single state. And why not? Did Jesus say that everyone must get married? The answer is that he didn't. He didn't get married himself. Does that make him less of a man? Finally, and at the end of the day, marriage is about having children. There is no doubt in my mind that children need the strong security that a mother and father loving each other can provide. But why should every woman have to bear children? She is biologically made to have them, but does that mean that she must have them? When I was younger, if I had worked and trained night and day to make it possible for me to run a four-minute mile, I believe I could have done it. I had all the necessary component parts to do it. But I chose not to. I don't sit in a lather of guilt and frustration because I didn't choose to do it. So there are perfectly normal human beings who don't get married. Their choice of celibacy is healthy and not anti-life.

The problem arises for a man or woman who desperately wants to be married, but who has never been asked, or has not been able to accept the invitation to go ahead. Herein lies the pain of loneliness. The years tick by and the looks of a woman deteriorate, and she fears that her chances of winning a man are gone for ever. The man gets so set in his ways that he could never share a home with a woman, even a saint would irritate him to distraction because he thinks he could do all those things better for himself.

So we have lonely bachelors who really only want women on their own terms, and man-hating women who are blaming men or themselves for their loneliness.

I am not concerned with marriages that do work. Nor with women or men who can manage alone, they are all right and can look after themselves. The people I care about are those who are trapped in a marriage that is dead. Or people who live alone longing to find a mate and either can't find one or don't bother to look.

CHAPTER 4

Another Cause of Loneliness: The Investment Game

I spoke earlier of men who had invested their identity in their job, for example a docker who for 35 years had worked on the docks and then been faced with redundancy. It is a very destructive experience. Men invest their identity in their job. To a lesser extent they invest their identity in their marriage or their children but more of that later.

But to be out of work; it comes at two levels: those who are young and can't find work, and those who have worked for 30 years or more and are now not wanted.

I was 17. It was 1938. I hated the idea of war. At the time I was working as an office boy in Manchester. I wasn't really an *office* boy, I was a kind of postman. I delivered letters all over Manchester for my firm, to save the cost of postage. My wages were seventeen shillings a week in old money, something like 85p in new money. Because I hated the idea of war I spent a lot of time in the office arguing against the idea of it. The manager of the firm found out what I was doing and promptly gave me the sack. I should add that when the war came I volunteered for the Royal Air Force and served for five and a half years. So much for youthful idealism.

However, I was sacked. Out of work as I was, I travelled into Manchester every day with people who had jobs to go to. As we all got out of the train, 'they' disappeared down the rabbit-holes where their work awaited them. I was left in Piccadilly, with no hole to go down. It was dreadful to stand alone amidst people rushing off to work, being the only one with no job to go to. I felt desolated. If you have never been out of work you cannot begin to feel what it is like to have no work to go to. You feel cast out of society. You don't belong to the human race. You are an anonymous nobody. And if you are married when this happens to you, you feel a total failure because you can't provide adequately for your wife and family.

In many, many ways a man's identity resides in his job. 'I am a bricklayer' or 'I am a docker' or 'I am a car mechanic' or 'I am the Prime Minister'. Almost all men invest their identity in their work.

Women have a similar problem. They may be 'Women's Lib' and if so they invest their identity in the fact that they are like men in the work they do. If women aren't the liberated kind and they don't go out to work, then their identity resides in being a wife or a mother.

Take the last of these, being a mother. So many women invest their identity in being a mother. When the children grow up and leave the nest, if the mother's identity rests in the activity of mothering her children, when the children leave home she hangs on to them by using guilt–making ploys like 'When are you coming to see me?' or 'I am lonely, please come to see me'.

I had a friend whose mother insisted on his sending his washing to her right through the war. Doing his washing helped her to retain her identity as a mother. I had another friend who was internationally known as a preacher, who told me that he never realized that when his children left home his wife would be left empty, with no role, and she almost ceased to be a human being. Another friend, who knew a little more than my preacher friend, bought his wife a colour television set to make up for the loss of their only child.

What I am saying is that almost everyone invests their identity in their work, their marriage or their parental role. What happens to a human being when the role no longer exists? They feel bereft, lonely and unwanted.

Jesus said that it is folly to invest in the treasures of this world (money, family, status, job) because you can lose them all. He told the story of the rich farmer who had to build bigger and bigger barns to store his harvest, but, Jesus said, 'Tonight your soul will be required of you, what use will your well-stocked barns be to you then?'

The man in the Old Testament called Job had a lovely family, a lot of land, a lot of cattle, and he loved God as well. The devil said to God, 'No wonder Job loves you, look how well he is doing'. And the devil asked God if all that Job had could be taken away from him. God said that the devil could take away everything, except Job's soul. And Job lost everything except his soul. Did that destroy the person whose name was Job? No.

It is terrible to lose your job. It is terrible to lose your husband or wife. It is very hard to let your children go free. Why? Because we all invest who we are in the role of having a job, or having people who depend on us, or having people who love us, or in the possession of what we own.

I had a friend who had the finest private library I had ever seen. He loved his books. He fondled his books like a mother fondles a child. Every one of his books was like a child. He didn't just look at them. He read them. I met him when I was a young man and every week I went to see him and I observed what his books meant to him. He wasn't a miser. He chose and lent me one book every week. He chose it with care, and from him I was introduced to the wonderful world of literature. And then his sight began to go. And I watched him disintegrate, for what he had invested his identity in was no longer of any use.

I am 56 and most of my closest friends are in that age bracket. One by one they seem to be dying off. Why? I wonder if it is because they had reached what they aimed for. They had invested their identity in reaching their goal and having reached it they had nothing left to live for. They had struggled to build up for themselves 'treasure in this world' and having got the treasure, they found that they needed something more, something that didn't only belong to this world. Could it be that out of total frustration they died? I don't know. I simply ask.

I want to make their deaths worthwhile. I want to learn from them a lesson. A lot of my friends died in the last war, because they believed that by dying they would eradicate the personification of evil which was Hitler. So they died. But other 'Hitlers' have arisen. You can never win that game. Because for every Hitler you defeat another will rise in his place.

When I say that a lot of my friends died in that war I mean just that. Geoff Harrison who could have played for England at cricket. Geoff Goddard who was one of my closest friends. Tom Miller who cared about every person he met. Then there was my own brother who fought through Greece, and Crete and eventually arrived in North Africa as a marine, and then died.

But all these whom I loved died for what they believed in and I honour them, and I shed deep tears of sadness that they are gone. But the terrible question I have to ask is whether they died for the wrong cause? At the time I didn't think so. It is only in looking back I begin to wonder.

What is the cause for which you should live and if necessary die?

People will die for the plot of land that they call their own. People will wage verbal or physical warfare in order to protect that in which they have invested their soul. But:

'The Son of Man had nowhere to lay his head.'

'Sell all that you have and give to the poor,' said Jesus.

'If you love your parents or children or your friends more than you love me, then you have missed what it is all about,' said Jesus.

So where, I muse to myself, do you who are reading this, invest your self?

Is it in a husband whose loss would leave you empty and desolate? Or in a wife whose loss you would feel the same about?

Is it in a job which, if you lost it, would make you feel a useless no-good, an outcast?

Is it in a status (I am a shop steward, a husband or wife, a director, a Lord, a Queen, a father or mother, a child, a person approved of)? If it is in any of these or any others that you can think of, you are backing a loser because all of these can be taken away. What was going on in the mind of Marie Antoinette, the Queen of France, when she laid her head on the block of the guillotine? What use was her queenship then?

Four years ago when I had a bit of money I took my family to Elba, the place where Napoleon was exiled after his first capture. He still played the role of the Emperor, he was the lord of Elba. From Elba he planned his return as Emperor of France. He returned to France and waged war against all his enemies. He had to be the Emperor of the whole world. But he lost at Waterloo and was deported to the island of St Helena in the middle of the Atlantic. He died there, lonely and disillusioned and probably the victim of syphilis. But how ironic that he died on an island named after the woman who spent her life looking for the cross of Jesus, the only thing that could have helped him (but more of that later).

So we all play games. We all have a role and we strive with all the power we have got to keep the role intact. But all these roles are vulnerable, they are all open to be attacked or destroyed. Suppose you have invested who you are in a role, then when the role is taken away, or quite simply dies, who are you going to be then?

It is always tragic when parents invest their longing to be successful in their children. I wonder how many doctors have sons who are doctors? How many clergymen have sons who are clergymen? Politicians with sons who are in politics? Miners whose sons go down the pit with them? Why do parents live their lives through their children?

Out of misplaced filial loyalty, children grow up to fulfil their parents' dreams. I remember one young man whose father desperately wanted him to be a doctor. For six years the son slogged away at medical subjects in which he hadn't got the slightest interest. The son was a misfit, training for a role he just didn't want to occupy. Eventually the son gathered all his moral strength together and announced to his father that he was giving up medicine. I know just how much it cost that son to tell his father that. Soon afterwards, the father died, and at the funeral the father's brother told me that the son had driven his father to his grave. What a terrible thing to say. What a mountain of guilt fell on that poor son's head. His father, instead of finding fulfilment in his own self-hood, needed the son's self-hood in order to survive. The end of that story is that the son eventually found a career that expressed who he was and I have reason to believe that he is a thousand times happier than he would have been if he had acted out his father's dreams.

I have known many spinsters so tied by a demanding parent that they have given up any hope of personal fulfilment. They have bodies that no man has been allowed to love because the parental possessiveness demanded the body and soul of the daughter. Such parents should be seen for what they are, blood-sucking leeches. Unable to face life on their own they suck their children dry in order to avoid the pilgrimage into aloneness. And when the parents die the grown-up children are too old then to make a new life of their own, and their *raison d'être* dies with the death of the parent. I think of one woman who shared her married home with her mother. The mother was imperious, demanding, autocratic. The daughter and her husband spent all their married life placating the unceasing demands of the mother. Towards the end of her life the mother could only walk with the aid of a stick and I can recall the mother saying to the daughter, 'Don't throw this stick away when I die, because soon after my death you will need it'. How right she was. The daughter and her husband only had a few weeks together after the mother died before she developed terminal cancer. I sat with that daughter towards the end as she poured out her hate and anger for a mother who, like a vampire, had destroyed her. Loneliness? Oh yes, the mother was lonely all right and she needed her daughter to ease the pain. The daughter was lonely because there was no room for her and her husband to live a life together. Three terribly lonely people living together, each in their own way suppressing a hate that couldn't be expressed. The end of that story is that the husband who never had a wife that he could call his wife, soon followed both of them to the grave. Three people who had never lived, now dead.

It is a terrible story, but it is going on all the time. Parents terrified of being left alone, sucking out the blood of their grown-up children. I don't blame those parents, I don't blame the children. Each is the victim of not being able to stand alone. The parent horrified by the thought of loneliness, the child overwhelmed with guilt if he refuses to co-operate with the parent's demands.

Is there another way? Yes, there is.

CHAPTER 5

Loneliness: The Feeling of Isolation

In 1974 I went to work in Zambia. I was the only white person in the firm. It was a mind-bending experience. No one was unkind to me, yet I never felt that I belonged. Zambia is independent, ruled by a black man, Kenneth Kaunda, one of the kindest and most generous people you could wish to meet. All offices of state were occupied by black Zambians (there may have been some white statesmen but I never saw or met them). It was very strange to walk about in Zambia and experience what it is like to belong to a minority. Until this happened to me I had no idea how coloured people feel who live in Britain. Coloured people who live here have to adjust to the British way of life. White people in Zambia have to adjust to the Zambian way of life. It is stupid to say that we are all the same. We are not, and thank God we aren't. Adjusting to another culture, another way of life, another way of thinking is painfully difficult; but apart from nationalistic morons, who are isolated within their jingoism, the differences have to be recognized and understood, and that leads to enrichment.

We ought to be able to do this. After all, the biggest difference we have to cope with is that between male and female and some people manage to make a union out of that difference. Even so the black-white differences are plaguing a great part of Africa. In Zambia I felt isolated and this was not due to any unkind arrogance on the part of the black people. It was my fault for being so caught up in the white way of life, the white way of thinking, and white cultural values.

The feeling of isolation was very real. I suppose that Jews have felt this for centuries. 'No man is an island', said John Donne. Well, he's not in the sense that the way he behaves affects other people. Yet in another sense each man and woman *is* an island. No matter how well I know you there is no way in which I can get inside you and have your thoughts or your feelings. You can tell me the last, minute detail about how you 'tick' but finally it is you that *know* how you 'tick', it is you that think your thoughts, you who feel your feelings. I get irritated by people who say to me, 'I know how you are feeling'. They don't know how I am feeling. When I have had toothache I have wished that someone could share the pain, but they can't. The toothache is mine and cannot be shared.

There are enough reasons for isolation that cannot be avoided, without our inventing more. But we invent them all the time. Usually we isolate people because they are different. Black people aren't white so they cannot be one of us who are white. Women aren't men so they can't be one of us because we're men. Roman Catholics aren't Protestants so they can't be one of us because we are Protestants. Homosexuals can't be one of us because we are normal. Normal! What on earth is normal? You can't be one of us because you have been to prison. You can't be one of us because you had to be put into a mental hospital. I've been a patient in a mental hospital three times so I can't be one of 'you'. I have no right to be inviting you to read this book because you must be thinking that I am a 'nut', and therefore cannot possibly have anything worthwhile to say.

Talking about being a 'nut', which I suppose I am, let me tell you about visiting day in a mental hospital. I rarely got a visit because the hospital was a long way from my home, and my wife, bless her, had two children to look after. So, often on visiting days, I sat in the canteen alone and observed the 'nuts', of whom I was one, talking with the visitors. It was a very big hospital and I didn't know all the patients by sight. I observed the small groups sitting round the separate tables. I promise you that except in a very few instances it was impossible to pick out the 'nuts' from the 'normals'. When visiting time ended and the visitors made their preparations for leaving, I was often confounded because the people that I had guessed were the 'nuts' were in fact the 'normals' and were going back into society. 'Poor old society,' I used to think, 'with all these nutty-normals as part of normal life.' Once in mental hospital I went for a long walk outside the grounds (with the doctor's permission!) and when I turned to go back realized that I was very tired. So I thumbed a lift. A car stopped and I got in. 'Where are you going?' the driver asked. 'To the lunatic asylum,' I replied. I watched the speedometer climb from forty to sixty! So many jobs are closed to me because I was once classed as a mental hospital patient, which I was, and might be again. What us 'nuts' know though is that most 'normals' are even 'nuttier' than we are. But the isolation game goes on. 'Oh! he went into mental hospital did he, I see, well, you'd better keep a careful eye on him.' Field Marshal, Earl Douglas Haigh sent tens of thousands of soldiers to be slaughtered for no sane reason that most military historians can discern, but that didn't mean that he was classed as out of his mind.

I've forgotten the name of the man who, a few years ago, was nominated to be Vice-President of the USA, but when it was discovered that long ago he had been helped by a psychiatrist he was dropped like a red-hot potato, so that today I can't even remember his name.

Three years ago I was interviewed for the job of prison chaplain. I knew a lot about prisons and about criminals, and I accept that some people must be kept out of society because of the terrible things they do within it. However, if you are born into a family who are criminals and your boyhood friends come from families who are criminals then you haven't much chance of keeping out of crime yourself. So, with a background of mental hospital treatment, and the fact that I said at the interview that I was on the side of the under-dog, I wasn't surprised that I was turned down for the job. It did not make me feel bitter, but it did encourage me to question how the person who has not known isolation can minister to the person who is going through it.

There are so many people who, because they feel that they are not quite normal, think that if society knew about them then society would discard them.

Let me give a word of comfort to any readers who feel that if the truth about them was known, then they would be shunned. There is no such person as the normal human being. I've travelled a lot of the world and I've met and known intimately the highly born and the lowly born, and I have yet to meet the normal human being. I've met the Christian, the agnostic and the atheist, and they are all thoroughly mixed up human beings. The Christians who treat their faith seriously will admit to their confusion. The agnostic and the atheist are in a much more perilous condition. Christians who are worth the name will echo the words of the man in the New Testament who said, 'Lord, I believe, help thou my unbelief'. But atheists give me the impression that they must keep their atheism going at all costs. I do not believe that their atheism is rational. I believe that they have an enormous emotional and personal investment in their position as atheists.

In the last few years I have become increasingly aware that teenagers feel the desolation of isolation. How do you explain the rise in football hooliganism? The soaring incidence of mindless vandalism? The almost total anti-social behaviour of vast numbers of young people? They feel that they just do not belong. They feel that they are simply not wanted. So, they lash out, they smash, they wreck and injure. Why? They are protesting against a society that has shown quite clearly that they are not wanted. To leave school as one of 1,400 school-leavers when the Labour Exchange has only 30 jobs on offer (as happened recently in one borough I know) can only be seen as saying, 'Clear off, we don't want to know you'. I heard that in some cases Careers Officers don't visit schools, because the very fact that their visit might imply that there are careers open to be pursued may give the school-leavers a false impression. If this book is read at all widely there will be a rush of pundits who, like a charge of wild elephants, will advance on me to trample me down with a million facts and figures. That will not alter the fact that we have educated young people for jobs that don't exist or have failed to educate them for jobs that do.

So the 'young' are feeling isolated. They are 'us' against 'them'. 'How can I even think of getting married,' said one 18-year-old boy to me the other day, 'when there is not the slightest hope of getting a job that could support a wife and family?' So for him women aren't people from whom you choose one to marry, with whom together you can find joy and happiness and fulfilment. Women are just things who are useful to prove that your manliness is still intact. And society isn't a lot of individual human beings who have their problems like you have yours, they are 'them', to be vandalized, mugged or robbed as the desire arises to do it.

We (that means you and I) have isolated so many human beings; the blacks or the whites, the mentally ill, the homosexual, the vandal, the criminal, the divorced, the illiterate, the foreigner, the people of another class, the house owner, the one who pays rent, the church-goer and the non-church-goer. We have put everyone into a category and relate only to those who are in the category that we approve of. I tell you that if you pursue that road you will relate to only one person and that is you, and you will know deep loneliness – superior, looking down on the rest of us idiots who do not match the standards that you have set.

Or (and this is important), you will feel so dreadfully unimportant that you will feel unworthy to relate to anyone else. I just don't know which is worse, to scorn the rest of humanity because you feel that they are not worthy of you, or to feel so inferior that you are not fit to be recognized by the rest of the human race.

In addition to knowing what it is like to be a patient in a mental hospital, I have more than the average knowledge of what it is like to be in prison. At the moment there are 40,000 men and women in prison. Many more men than women. Why is that? I have often wondered.

I was an acting prison chaplain in 1953. In more recent years I have visited prisoners in Walton (Liverpool);

Thorpe Arch, near Leeds; Pentonville, Wormwood Scrubs, and Holloway (women only) in London; Eastchurch in Kent; and Ford in Sussex. In addition, one of my uncles was a prison chaplain for something like 20 years.

There are four reasons given for putting people in prison. The first is that the experience inside prison will reform the prisoner. It may in some cases. On the other hand it could make the man or woman concerned more anti-social than ever. The second argument is that the threat of prison will deter people who are tempted to break the law. It may deter some, but why do others go back to prison time and time again? For some reason, when we look back we seem to erase from the memory what was dreadful. I served for five and a half years in the RAF, in the war. I went through some terrible experiences but I never dwell on them, it is the good times I remember most often. The third reason for putting people in prison is quite simply punishment. 'An eye for an eye, a tooth for a tooth.' A form of revenge. That is the view of Edgar Lustgarten. He would hang people for murder. I disagree completely with him but I do admire his openness. He does not cloud his simple view that wrongdoers should be punished, with unreal talk about reforming or deterring. The fourth reason for prison, and the only one I can go along with, is that some people must be kept out of society. The criminally insane. I don't just mean those who are technically in a legal sense insane, but those for whom violence is a way of life. Those who see bad as good and are hell-bent on destroying people and society. But to keep such people out of society doesn't mean putting them into what we now call prison, for the rest of their lives.

It costs something like £80 a week to keep someone in prison. I doubt if that money is being spent wisely. I would have thought that once you have rejected the notion of prison as revenge in a civilized society, then you must feel considerable unease about what we do with men and women, boys and girls who have been found guilty of breaking the law and been sent to prison, borstal or detention centre.

Even from a selfish point of view we should want the

lawbreaker who has acted against society to learn how to live within society. And what do we in fact do to achieve this laudable end? We separate these people from society, isolate them from normal life and then have the mad idea that we will, by doing that, achieve our desired purpose.

I have observed with my own eyes the boy who first broke the law and was fined. Broke the law again and went to borstal. Broke the law again and went to detention centre. Broke the law again and went to prison, and as far as I know today, that ghastly treadmill continues to grind on and on. If ever a system could be devised that helped a person, on being asked the question 'Who are you?', to answer 'I have no place in society', then our penal system is the ideal one for evoking that response.

I am not judging the judges who send people to prison; they simply carry out the rules of the system that we allow. Mind you, because a judge has the power, in some cases to send a person to prison or award a suspended sentence, or even determine the length of the sentence, I'm not at all sure that he is the right person to do that. Let the judge 'try' the case in a legal sense by all means, but when it comes to dealing with the guilty person I have grave doubts that the judge is at all fitted to do it. I mentioned this matter to a lawyer once and I was amazed when he said, 'Of course the judges are the right people to decide the future of the guilty. Judges know the criminal mind better than anyone.' That really is nonsense. Assuming that some people who break the law are illiterate, come from a criminal background, received inadequate schooling, lived their lives in a socially deprived, over-crowded area (where I live in East London, or Everton in Liverpool, or Bethnal Green, or the middle of Birmingham, etc., etc.), what judge in the whole of Britain can even begin to understand the mind of such people, never mind understand how to decide their future? I would be surprised to hear the name of one judge who does not come from a background of privilege. The judges, however, have the power to send people to prison.

The first thing that happens when you begin your sentence is that your own clothing is taken away and you are given a prison uniform. Then your name becomes of little importance, you become a number. You are no longer John, you are '300,019'. Who are you? A 'number', dressed and looking like all the other 'numbers'.

The whole prison system is designed to de-humanize the people 'inside'. Is it surprising that many of these 'numbers' are unable to relate to a society made up of persons when they are released?

Come with me to a prison I know on visiting day. A canteen filled with small tables. Round each table is grouped the prisoner and his friends and family, averaging four people. Husbands with wives. Fathers with children. All of them treasuring every second of the 30 minutes allowed for a visit. Two visits a month. Husbands holding their wives' hands or touching their knees. At the end of the visit a kindly prison officer signals the end of the time. One last kiss for the woman he loves, a hug for the children and they are gone for another fortnight. He goes back to his isolation and she to hers. I'm not quite sure whose is the harsher punishment, the husband's 'inside' or the wife's at home.

What about the victims of crime? My compassion for them is as great as yours. However, that doesn't alter at all my deep conviction that prison is wrong.

What is the alternative? I do not know. However, until enough of us are convinced that prison is a useless method of dealing with criminals and say so, there will be no motivation for people wiser than I am to find a better way.

I suppose that there were people in the nineteenth century who argued that the British economy would collapse without the slave trade; that could have been the case but slavery was still wrong.

A friend who read the first draft of this book said that it wasn't good enough to condemn the present prison system without saying something about how things could be altered. I hesitate to do this because I am not an expert criminologist or penologist, I am just an amateur, but I have had a lot of experience of prisons and prisoners. So very diffidently I am willing to make a few suggestions.

I believe that we should give every kind of backing to

methods of dealing with criminals other than sending them to prison. There are judges willing to try other alternatives. Community service is one such. A person is sentenced to so many hours, with a maximum of 240, working for the community. The person who truly regrets having offended against society is thereby given the chance to put back into society what he has taken away. The hostel system could be encouraged. This system gives to selected people the choice of prison or living in a hostel, going out to work, earning their keep, and under the kindly supervision of a hostel warden learning how to live without breaking the law.

Some believe that by making prison harder, tougher, more frightening, then people would hesitate longer before breaking the law. This would not and does not work. The men I have talked to who have been serving prison sentences all say that the only punishment that really affects them is the loss of liberty. The hardness or softness of the life inside prison has very little effect. If that is indeed the case, then confinement could be right, but what happens within that confinement becomes of paramount importance. Not the hardness or the softness but the way that the time is spent. Can it do any other than damage to a person who from three months to ten years has his life filled with what is boring, uncreative and to a large extent non-productive? This is little more than a long period of training in how to be a useless member of society.

If we are really concerned about the effects of criminality upon society, should we not be much more concerned than we are with what we are training locked-up people to become? The young men in my neighbourhood who go to prison, or detention centre or borstal, are not afraid of it at all. They are very tough, and making confinement tougher will only make them harder. Have we the patience, even the desire, to offer to people in confinement alternatives to a challenge to beat the system? For that is what the young men around here feel. The police are a challenge to be defeated. Confinement is a challenge to survive, and they come out even more determined to carry on challenging the system. Suppose the system worked *for* them instead of against them? Not for them in the sense of making them harder, but letting them discover that there was more to life than simply having to smash, destroy, grab or be one up.

This approach would require another kind of prison officer than the type we recruit. The present officers are chosen and trained to keep the present system going. Many of them would gladly work another system, but the rules within prison don't allow it. A good teacher sets out to win the respect of his class and from that there flows obedience. A repressive teacher is only adding further pressure to the seeds of the natural rebellion that are already there. I get weary of listening to those who moan on and on about the increase in crime, and fail to see that apart from increased detection a great deal more money would have to be spent in selecting, training and paying prison officers who would be able to do more than is done now to ensure that a man who goes to prison once would never go again. I do not know the statistics but I would hazard the guess that the majority of people who are undergoing confinement are not doing so for the first time. I write this at a time when George Davies, a notorious East End criminal, released from prison after a massive campaign that protested his innocence, is now back in custody charged with armed bank robbery. Was anything done, apart from confinement, to ensure that he would not break the law again? Confinement alone will not do that. Repressive measures inside prison would not do that. There simply must be another way.

CHAPTER 6

Loneliness Caused by Guilt

Thirty years ago, a friend called John Smith (that really is his name, and he is a teacher in York) said to me, 'Guilt rules the world'. It meant nothing to me then. In those days I would have said that sex ruled the world and Freud would have agreed. Or I might have said that thirst for power ruled the world, and Adler, who was a psychologist of the same era as Freud and taught that everyone was driven by the need for power, would have agreed.

Sex and power and aggression seemed to me, thirty years ago, to be the driving force for most people.

However, I now believe that John Smith had reasons for saying what he did. Guilt isolates. Guilt cuts you off from other people. Guilt creates terrible loneliness. Guilt causes violence.

How can a wife who despises her husband and yet can see his need to be loved, ever tell him what she thinks and feels? So she has to pretend, and suffer the guilt for her pretence. She could, of course, tell him and that could help him to change, but the shock of what she would tell him might drive him to suicide or some lesser form of self-destruction. So her guilt grovels on.

I remember the first time that I caressed a woman. I was 22, she was 20. I loved her. We were alone, during the war, on a secluded beach near Karachi in India. It was a Sunday afternoon and I was due to preach that night in a local church. Later, when I stood in the pulpit, I felt like a leper. I felt totally and completely unworthy of standing in the pulpit proclaiming the love of Jesus. What was wrong about what I had done? Today it would be considered innocent, but it felt wrong. I had done it because I loved her, but having done it I felt like an outcast.

Guilt comes in many different ways, and each way causes a terrible feeling of loneliness, the feeling that you are cut off from the rest of the human race.

When Judas realized what his betrayal of Jesus really meant, he thought there was only one thing left for him to do. He went and committed suicide.

Guilt is so universal, as John Smith said. You are a man but your mother wanted a girl so you feel guilty about being a man, or you are a woman but your mother wanted a boy so you feel guilty about your womanhood.

You are happy as a machine tool operator but your parents wanted you to work in a bank, and your feelings of guilt for not fulfilling your parents' dreams make it impossible for you to enjoy what you are doing. Or you obey the authority figure and do what is demanded and for ever after feel unfulfilled and resentful.

'These soldiers are nailing me to this cross,' said Jesus, 'but please forgive them, it's not really their fault.' I wonder if they realized that he meant it?

I am not against the Roman Catholic Church. I suspect though that what people confess in those little wooden confessional boxes isn't what they really feel guilty about. 'I missed Mass last Sunday.' 'I got drunk last Friday.' 'I had a fight last Thursday.' 'I have masturbated three times since my last confession.' Are those the things that the priest hears? I'm not knocking the idea of confession. On the contrary I only wish that there could be more, but more of the real thing. The real guilt hangs like a ball and chain round our ankles, and impedes our involvement now in the joy that life can offer, and as it ties us with unbreakable bonds to the past, so it spoils all happy expectations of the future.

Shakespeare got it right when he described Lady Macbeth. She helped her husband to commit murder, and the guilt for what she had done obsessed her. Although she must have washed a thousand times, in her guilt-tortured mind she could still see the blood stains on her wrists. Night after night she walked the castle corridors gazing at the imagined blood stains on her arms, crying out 'Out, out damned spot, out I say', but the blood stains remained. Observing her from an alcove as she passed, her doctor said 'More needs she the divine than a physician'.

It was in loneliness that she walked. We all walk in loneliness with our guilt, and for some people such as Lady Macbeth, madness is the end-product.

If you and I met, there are things about you that you wouldn't tell me. Some of these things are private and belong only to you or to one other person, and that is right and proper. There are other things though that you wouldn't share with another living soul. Why? Because you feel that you would lose the esteem in which they held you. In many cases you would be wise to keep your own counsel, because the person with whom you might share your deepest guilt would write you off. So you must hug your guilt to your own breast and suffer the tortures of the damned in your loneliness.

The strange thing is though that what I think is completely beyond forgiveness could be for someone else quite easily forgivable. I have heard hundreds of confessions in my time. In my early years people who came to make their confession sometimes began with the preamble, 'You'll never speak to me again when you've heard what a terrible, horrible, miserable sinner I am'. In those early years, I used to brace myself in case I heard something so terrible that I would fall back in shock and horror. There they were, locked up in the agony of their guilt and loneliness, and I used to wonder how I could go on loving them having heard what monsters they were in their private, secret, lonely lives. And what did I hear when at last the terrible secret shames were revealed? I was young, and therefore you must try to understand that I expected something really terrible. But the confessions didn't shock me, with all my youthful lack of experience of what men and women could do if they sank into total depravity. What I heard was something so ordinary, so banal that I was actually disappointed. I had hoped for something much worse!

Now, of course I know that the causes of guilt in people are not what I think should cause them to feel guilty, it is what causes guilt in them. That's what matters. I have learned also that guilt, no matter what its cause, separates us from the rest of mankind. It is like moral leprosy, making us feel unfit to associate with other people.

A whole book could be written about why people feel guilty and why a lot of the guilt is unnecessary. On the other hand some people have every reason to feel guilty and they need the forgiveness of God. My concern here, though, is for people who feel guilty without sufficient cause for their guilt. Do you think it is wrong to eat meat? Ghandi ate meat when, as a young man, he was studying law in England, and he was overwhelmed with guilt. Was his guilt appropriate? A young man told me the other day that he felt guilty and ashamed because he couldn't relate to girls of his own age. Was his guilt necessary? A father who works all the hours he can, to provide for his family, told me that he felt guilty because in spite of all his efforts he couldn't provide what he thought was enough. Is his guilt justified?

Guilt comes in many forms, but it is always accompanied by feelings of loneliness.

Is there anyone with nothing to hide? I doubt it. I'm not pleading for a mass confession of secret guilt, justified or not. What I am saying is that everyone has their secret store of guilt and because of its existence everyone experiences a corresponding sense of loneliness.

It is not by chance that at the heart of the Christian message Jesus called (and calls) for people everywhere to repent and accept forgiveness. It is obvious to me that Jesus knew that eating at the heart of every human being like a cancer lies a burden of guilt, which can be healed by the word of forgiveness.

Why do we allow our guilt to cut us off from a completely open relationship with our closest friends? The reason is so obvious it is hardly worth stating. However, it must be spelled out because so many people don't act upon it. We keep our guilt to ourselves because we are deeply afraid that if we shared it with someone we loved they would cease to love us. That is why we hug our guilt to our own breast. We are afraid that we would forfeit love if we made known the whole truth about us. So much for what we call being loved.

If you start by assuming that no one is perfect then how can you be shocked when you find out that they are not? That does not mean that it is right to condone sin. What it does mean is that none of us can set himself up as the judge of others, and the last thing any of us has the right to do is to condemn another human being. We are all guilty. We all stand in need of forgiveness.

'Forgive us our trespasses as we forgive those who trespass against us,' says the Lord's Prayer. 'Neither do I condemn you,' said Jesus. 'Go and sin no more,' he said to the woman who had committed adultery.

Stay within the isolation of your guilt if that is what you choose. Present a guilt-free face to the world if you can't trust in forgiveness, and let the cancer of secret guilt eat away at your soul.

But neither should we parade our guilt and wallow in it publicly. That is simply obnoxious and infinitely boring.

Just quietly and humbly share your guilt with someone who can accept it and not be damaged by it. Then the prison cell opens and you can walk out into the clean, fresh air, free, free to love and free to be loved, with the future offering a new beginning.

At the heart of the Christian Gospel is the cross. That cross is God's way of saying that if you are truly and honestly sorry for what you have done wrong, then forgiveness and freedom from guilt are yours. It puzzles me why so many people ignore this priceless gift.

It is also strange that so many people who know that the Gospel is about forgiveness just cannot believe that such forgiveness is for them. John Bunyan and John Wesley were both plagued with the conviction that they could not be forgiven. When at last the realization that they were forgiven entered their tortured minds, they became new men with a gospel of liberation for tens of thousands of people.

When the preacher says, 'If you repent and mean it you will receive forgiveness', he means *you.*

You, reading these words now. You can be freed from guilt. I know of no other words to convince you that this is true.

'Dear Jesus, help me to understand and to accept that no matter what my sins are you will meet my repentance with love, acceptance and forgiveness.'

CHAPTER 7

Loneliness — at the Top and at the Bottom

It was Harry Truman, one-time President of the United States, who said 'the buck stops here'. There are not many people who can say that in such a complete sense. In spite of all the advice, support and encouragement he might have received, the decision to drop the atom bomb on Hiroshima in 1945 was finally his. There was no one else to whom he could give the responsibility of deciding. If the whole world had been destroyed because of that decision the responsibility for making it was his. I wonder how deep his loneliness was at that time?

The higher you climb in any sphere of life, the lonelier it becomes. To be on the top of any human heap is to have no equals with whom to share the loneliness of that summit. I remember when I was involved in re-building a church in Guildford and there was a site foreman. Day after day he had to make many decisions. He had to plan the progress of the work. He had to order the bricks, the cement, the sand, the wood at just the right time so that there was no hold-up in the work. He had to employ tradesmen on exactly the day when they would be needed. And I noticed that there was a strange barrier between him and the other men. It wasn't that he was unfriendly or difficult to get on with. It was that the other men recognized that he was the decision-maker and it set him apart. At the opening celebrations of the finished church we presented him with a present. Why him? Because we recognized that although all the men had worked hard and well for us, he had carried a special burden, and that was the burden of being the leader of the work force, and leadership in all its forms means being out there on your own, and our present to that site foreman was our way of recognizing this.

Research scientists must have this experience of being out there on their own. Albert Einstein, although married, with a family, lived apart from them, and in addition there was no other human being around who could share with him his excitement when he discovered that $E=MC^2$. I have a relative who is an expert in switch-gear. A switch breaks the electric current, creating a gap that the electricity cannot jump. But what happens when the electrical power is thousands of times greater than our ordinary domestic electrical power? An ordinary switch will not break the current. It can only be broken in a bath of oil. When the current breaks, a bubble is formed. My relative did the thesis for his doctorate on what went on inside the bubble when the current was broken! He had to be examined on his thesis, and there were only two men in the whole of Britain who knew enough about that bubble to ask him any questions on his thesis, and they didn't know as much as he did. His book is still the standard work on the oil bath bubble. In those days he was on his own.

With whom did Isaiah share his vision in the Temple? Who would have understood? When Martin Luther said, 'Here I stand, I can do no other', one gets the impression that he was standing alone. When I read St Paul's letters I get the feeling that he was very much on his own even amongst his fellow Christians, because he spent so much time explaining to them truths that he had grasped and they hadn't.

We talk about 'mountain top' spiritual experiences, and what we mean is that they were peculiar to us, experiences that cannot be shared. When you are out there or up there on your own there are so many people who would be only too pleased to prove that you are mistaken. There is a nasty human tendency to want to drag down people who are above us, or drag back people who are in front of us. There is only one person who can be out there with you, understanding where you are and willing to stay with you whether you are right or wrong. There is only one person who can share your own personal summit without wanting to drag you down, and who will stay with you if you do have to come down. That person is Jesus. For he is both out in front and way above every one of us but also willing to be with us at the point we are at. A true companion indeed. It is not for nothing that we sometimes call him Lord of Lords, or King of Kings, or say that 'at the name of Jesus every knee shall bow'. It is only with him that we can survive the lonely or the heady experience of being on top or out in front. It is only with him that we can have the courage or be saved from the destructive conceit of being up there or out there on our own.

It is lonely also at the bottom. I was on Paddington station in London the other morning. It was 7 a.m. On one of the benches a down-and-out man was sleeping. Dressed in an old raincoat held together by a piece of string, with a brown paper parcel that contained all his worldly possessions being used as a pillow. Although it was 7 a.m. there were many people about, hurrying past him. He looked dreadfully lonely. I know many tramps, or wayfarers as I prefer to call them. They are all 'loners'. They sometimes work in teams to get food or alcohol but their relationships are always transient, they do not stay in the same place with the same person for very long. For reasons that I do not understand they have chosen loneliness as a way of life. They will tell you that they prefer it that way. But why do they need booze as soon as they waken? Because the isolation of their way of life cannot be faced with a mind that is sober.

When you are on the way up, there are many people who will attach themselves to you, but when you are on the way down it comes as quite a shock that people who wanted to know you on the way up don't recognize you when you are on the way down. At the bottom, unless you are peculiar like a wayfarer, you are just part of a faceless mass. There is nothing that makes you stand out from the others. You are just one of life's many failures lost in one great lump. As I write this we are in the middle of raging inflation and rising unemployment. There are a few who are able to weather this storm by keeping their jobs and having their wages linked to inflation, and in some cases even increasing their wages or salaries faster than inflation. But for the powerless, the faceless ones, despair deepens and anxiety mounts, and there is the dread of being lumped with all those others who have not been able to keep up.

I learned something quite shocking about myself on an occasion in Zambia. I was there to make some recordings for the BBC, and was asked if I would like to meet a leper. I accepted the invitation. It was arranged for me to meet him in a garden. I arrived early and was sitting on a garden seat. Eventually he came walking across the lawn to meet me. I stood up and instinctively stretched out my hand to shake his, and then in one fleeting moment I had a flash of fear. What could happen if I touched him? I didn't know then that you cannot catch leprosy by touch. It is caught by inhaling tiny globules of moisture in the breath.

One of the outstanding things about Jesus during his life on earth was the way that he treated every individual human being with respect. Not just the ones at the top but also the ones at the bottom, many of whom were obviously enduring that loneliness that comes to people who are at the bottom of the pile. Zacchaeus, a tax collector who although a Jew worked for the Romans who occupied the country and who was therefore hated and despised by his fellow countrymen – Jesus went to that man's house for a meal. He met a woman at a well and it was midday. A woman at a well at midday in those times was unusual. The women went for water during the cool of the early morning or the early evening. No woman would ordinarily go at midday when the heat from the sun was at its fiercest. Her reason for going to the well at that time could have been because she would have been ostracized by the women who went to the well at the usual times, and the reason for this became clear as Jesus talked to her. She was not respectable, she was promiscuous, and might even have been a prostitute. And not only that, she was a woman and Jesus was a rabbi and rabbis didn't speak to women in public. On top of all that, she was a Samaritan and the Jews, of whom Jesus was one, did not speak to Samaritans. There were so many reasons why in the presence of Jesus she should have felt right at the bottom of the pile. But he didn't react to her in that way; on the contrary he treated her as though she was the most important person in the world. He was at a dinner given in his honour by the people at the top. During the dinner a prostitute burst in and flung herself at his feet. All the other guests were shocked. But not Jesus. He treated her with infinite tenderness and afterwards was criticized for not shunning her. And there was a woman who was discovered committing adultery, and in accordance with the law of those days she should have been stoned to death. Jesus said to her, 'I don't condemn you, but don't do it again.' There was Peter who bravely followed after Jesus to the place where Jesus was under arrest, but at the last minute his nerve broke and he denied that he had ever known Jesus. Peter wept bitter tears of remorse because of what he had done. But it was Jesus who after his resurrection made the first move towards Peter, to help him out of the pit of shame into which he had fallen.

It is this same Jesus who is alive now who can meet us at the lowest point to which we may fall, and he meets us not with condemnation or arrogance, but with humility, compassion and even more important with accepting strength, sharing the pit with us until such time as we are ready to let him help us out of it into freedom and security.

There is one other matter I would like to raise. This may not apply to everyone but I know for a fact that it applies to some. There are people who, for reasons that are too complicated to go into now (and are not part of this book anyway), are afraid of success. People who are afraid to get to the top, who feel unentitled to be anywhere else but at the bottom of the pile. Such people if they do succeed will so order their lives that the top will become untenable. Underneath their success, which is valid and deserved, lies the dreadful feeling that it is undeserved. They live with success, expecting a thunderbolt to hit them and if it doesn't will manufacture a method that will lead to their downfall. It is the same with happiness. The same people feel utterly unentitled to live with peace of mind and the happiness that goes with it, and like conditioned robots will again so engineer their affairs as to make peace of mind and happiness impossible.

When I was 17 and had been preaching for a year I had a great desire to be as good a preacher as possible, but this desire became shrouded with guilt as I felt it was wrong to have such ambitions in a matter like preaching. I was in such distress that I arranged to see Dr Leslie Weatherhead, who at the time was one of the finest preachers in the world, but who was also a great pastor to the minds and souls of so many people. I explained my problem and with great tenderness he told me that it was not sinful or wrong to exercise to the full any gift or talent that God had given to me. It sounds so obvious, and yet to people who are afflicted with guilt at being any kind of a success it is not obvious at all. I have noted so many people who have got to the top or near to the top in their chosen calling, who have then engineered their own downfall which has led in some cases to self-destruction. Oscar Wilde, who was the greatest playwright of his day, chose to break the law as it then was and finished his life a broken man, a self-imposed exile from his own country. Dylan Thomas, whose poems and his play 'Under Milk Wood' still enchant us, drank himself to death. Did not Scott Fitzgerald, the American novelist, do the same? Horatio Bottomley, a prominent MP earlier this century, involved himself in a scandal that destroyed his career. 'Jimmy' Thomas, a Chancellor of the Exchequer, did the same. And what are we to say of President Nixon? There are many others. In every case as I observe them, I see as a component part of their self-destruction a strong element of the loneliness of being successful and at the top.

And one doesn't have to be a five-talented person to feel the loneliness of those talents that set you apart and lead you to breakdown. It can happen to people with fewer talents who, if they are exercised, go through the same fear of exercising them, and go to great lengths, either to see that they are not exercised or if they are, to see that they are not exercised for long.

Not all people who exercise their talents react in this

way, but many do. Jesus said that he had not come for the healthy but for the sick, not for the righteous but for the sinners. The person who can cope with success and being at the top is all right, it is those who cannot cope with it whom Jesus is able to help. He helps by calling us to use our talents, and to use them for him. Not to treat them as our own possessions to bring glory upon ourselves, but to use them as gifts from him to be used for him. In this attitude of humility we can use our talents without being destroyed by them. For many people these gifts are too powerful to be handled as possessions. They must be seen for what they are, gifts from him to be used for him. Only in that way can they be handled with safety and handled in such a way as to bring us fulfilment. The top of your summit is all right if you get there with him and stay there with him, otherwise what was meant by him to be a means of your fulfilment will become the cause of your destruction.

CHAPTER 8

Loneliness of the Disabled

It is probably presumptuous of me to write about the loneliness that some disabled people might feel, because I am not in any significant way disabled myself. I only have a functionally small amount of experience in this area. In recent months a cataract has grown over my right eye making it completely useless. A cataract is slowly forming on my left eye and until it is fully formed an operation is not possible. I do not know why this should be the case, the surgeon did explain but I failed completely to understand what he was telling me. However, I now find quite an amount of difficulty in seeing clearly. Being a keen sportsman I get frustrated at not being able to see the ball on television whilst watching cricket, tennis or golf. I pass people in the street who are on my right side and do not recognize them. People who are approaching me in the street I cannot see until they are on top of me, and if I know them well they are puzzled that I didn't smile with recognition when they were some distance away. And standing at request stops waiting for a bus, I cannot see its number until it is too late to hold out my hand. But as I said, this is a minor disablement compared with what some people have to cope with, but it has given me a tiny glimpse into their problem.

I have often wondered which would be worse, to go completely blind or stone deaf. I would prefer blindness. I can imagine that deaf people feel cut off in a way that blindness does not affect you. I find that with blind people I tend to raise my voice. It is stupid, but somehow my instinctive reaction to a blind person is to shout as though they can't hear. So no blind person would feel lonely with me, in fact they would feel quite the opposite, they would be anxious to get away. Complete deafness, however, would appear to me to cut you off from other people in a way that could be a much more miserable experience. To be able to see other people and not to be able to hear what they are saying I would find terribly frustrating. Is this why some partially deaf people become quite crotchety? They say with irritation, 'Speak up, speak up, I can't hear you'. I am not saying that blindness does not create very real problems and is not a heavy burden, I am simply saying that between deafness and blindness I would prefer not being able to see.

I had a very close friend who died slowly of muscular atrophy. It took him well over a year to die. It started almost unnoticeably when he found that he couldn't grip a golf club tightly. Then he began to stumble as he walked. It was dreadful to watch him as the disease slowly spread throughout his body. Towards the end it was awful. He was immobile. He had to be lifted from bed and put into a wheelchair, a wheelchair that he couldn't operate himself. He was totally dependent on other people pushing him about. Simple matters like going to the lavatory became great problems. If he was sitting on his own and needed the lavatory he had to wait until someone came into his room before he could be pushed to where he wanted to be. I try to imagine how desperately lonely a situation like that could be: to be utterly dependent on other people coming to you because you were completely incapable of going to them. And the terrible feelings of being a burden, of having to impose on other people's good nature. Such people (who avoid being utterly selfish and totally demanding) must go through many, many hours of abject loneliness as they try not to be a nuisance. Not that the people around them are unkind or thoughtless, but I can imagine the diffidence of some people who are disabled in this way about making their needs known.

It must be so easy when a disability strikes to sink into a deep state of self-pity or bitterness. I do not write that in any kind of critical or judging manner. I knew a salesman, who in middle life went totally blind. Until then he had been a very jovial out-going person, the life and soul of any party. His blindness changed him completely. He became sour and bitter, cursed God and cut himself off from the people who loved him the most. I did not blame him. I could not be sure that in his place I wouldn't have reacted in a similar manner.

Partial paralysis, or to lose a leg, must cut off the normal person from so much that he had taken for granted. Not to be able to join in. To be the odd one out when everyone around you is taking part in an activity that you are barred from must be very difficult. To be born disabled must have many problems, although it could be said that what you have never had you would not miss so much as to have had it and then to lose it.

How can those of us who are not disabled get into the minds of those who are? I don't think that we can. I have not always been as understanding as I might have been with some disabled people. I am not a very patient person. I don't find it easy to walk along very slowly if I am helping someone who is crippled to move from A to B. If only I could get into their minds I am sure that I would be much more patient and considerate. It has to be said that some of us are less kind than others.

But there is another side to disablement. Some people triumph over it in a most remarkable way. In my BBC days I met Group Captain Douglas Bader several times. He was involved in a flying accident before the war. He almost died, but with a supreme effort of will he resisted death. But he lost both his legs. I am awed by the courageous way he set about learning to walk with two artificial legs. By the time I knew him it was almost impossible to notice anything different in the way he walked from the walk of someone with two proper legs. No one knows the battles he must have fought and won within himself as he struggled to walk again. And with all the help that qualified people could give him, that battle I believe was won within the loneliness of his own heart and mind.

I know a man in broadcasting who every week presents a programme for the blind called 'In touch'. I don't know at what stage of his life he went blind, but what I do know is that he used his blindness and his victory over his handicap to minister to masses of people who had lost their sight. I have never known him to be any other than kind and gentle and considerate of other people. And what is more, he never lets his blindness embarrass other people. He taught me a lot, and I wonder if what he taught me I could have learned had he not been blind.

How should we who are not disabled react to those who are? Should we pretend that we have not noticed their disablement, in case it causes them to feel inadequate? I am sure that is not the way. I believe that such an attitude could only add to any loneliness that the disablement was already causing. It is similar to meeting someone who has recently been bereaved. Many people are embarrassed and do not know what to say to the bereaved one, so they don't mention it. But suppose that sad and broken person wants nothing more than to pour their heart out and release some of the pent-up loneliness? My way, for what it is worth, is always to recognize bereavement or disablement, because at least that is honest and the ensuing relationship can be true.

I hesitate to say this to disabled people, not having been seriously or permanently disabled myself. But I have a deep conviction that there is no situation that cannot be redeemed by Jesus Christ if it needs to be. I can only compare the loneliness of disablement with the loneliness that I have experienced in my own way. Looking back, I can see that because I offered what was happening to me to Jesus, now at last I can see that he used what at the time felt terrible, to enrich me and give me a much deeper understanding of people who were having to walk along the road that I had travelled.

I do not believe that God wills disablement. I believe that all forms of suffering are the result of the fallen world that we live in, or the result of our own fallen natures. It was this fallenness that Jesus came to redeem and I believe with all my heart that he can do it. The great secret is to be able to share it with him and to be able to offer it to him. Only this way can we be lifted out of the temptation to self-pity and bitterness. Only this way can what is not his will be transmuted into what can be used by him to enrich ourselves as people and to enrich other people. That is what David Scott Blackall of the BBC has done with his blindness. I do not know how much Christian faith Douglas Bader has, but I know that he has some. What I do believe is that it was the spirit of Jesus within him, plus his own courage, that got him through.

Dr W. E. Sangster, well known as one of the greatest preachers of this century, a man who revelled in his superb physical fitness, was struck down with a form of creeping paralysis. Eventually the paralysis affected his vocal chords and he was unable to speak. That wonderful, distinctive voice, that had thrilled 3,000 people week after week for many years at Westminster Central Hall, was now silent. But with his pen he spoke to countless people bringing them courage, hope and faith until the paralysis eventually killed him.

Someone who has been struck down, and through that has tasted the desolation of feeling that they do not belong to the normal human race, has a lot to give to the rest of us by entering the loneliness that ensues, grappling with it, defeating it, and being able to share with us what they have found.

CHAPTER 9

Loneliness — Existential Anxiety

Existential Anxiety? What a dreadful phrase. What could it mean? It is a phrase I first met when reading Paul Tillich, the American theologian-philosopher. On that first reading I had no idea what it meant. I know now what it means.

If I ask the question, 'Who are you?', and you can answer that question by saying, 'I am ME', you are well on the way to understanding what Existential Anxiety is all about. You are a Self who can feel happiness, sadness, acceptance, rejection, pain, anxiety, self-esteem, self-hatred, guilt, remorse, forgiveness, and so on. Within the body that I observe when I meet you, there is a registering agent. In Shakespeare's 'Merchant of Venice' Shylock, a Jew, tried to explain that Jews (who were then despised) were in fact persons or selves. Amongst other things, he said that if you stabbed him with a knife then just like other people he would bleed even though he was a Jew. Hitler tried to persuade his people that Jews weren't real human beings. The Hindus with their caste system still have the remains of an age-old belief that some people aren't really human and they are called 'outcasts'.

The truth is of course that every human being is human and each human being can say 'I am'. There are terrible forces at work in the world seeking to destroy the realization that everyone was created to say 'I am'.

Unwanted babies must find it very difficult to say 'I am', because in order to say 'I am' you first need someone else who says 'You are'. If someone else says 'You are' then it is possible for you to say 'I am'.

I believe that this process begins in the womb. I believe that the child in the womb knows whether it is recognized, wanted and treasured, or the reverse. I believe that abortion is a terrible act. It is like saying to a living self, not only are you unwanted, but you don't really exist. If those who believe that abortion is morally right would be prepared to say that destroying what is in the womb is a self, I don't think that there would be many abortions.

The struggle to be the self that you are is very difficult and very painful. Almost everyone around you demands that you be what *they* want you to be. Parents try to mould you to fit their wishes. Teachers try to fit you into the mould that they find tolerable. And society at large, with all its fears and anxieties, desperately needs you to conform to what they believe is the norm. What happens to the self that you are? In most cases it is never seen. What is seen is what you have been taught to be, what is acceptable, and those who have taught you that are those who in their turn weren't allowed to be who they are, but had to be what their society demanded that they should be. So, the game has gone on for century after century, everybody being persuaded to conform to what the society of the day found acceptable.

I am not talking now about the laws that are necessary to avoid chaos. Of course we must obey them. What I am talking about is the price you have to pay to affirm your self-hood with people who are afraid of what true self-hood is.

I remember a story of a tribe whose tribal call was a note played by blowing down a hollow reed that had one hole pierced in it. For centuries the tribe had used that one note. The day came when a young member of the tribe made two holes in a reed, and when he blew down it a different noise was heard. The tribe killed him. At all costs you must not be you. You must not be different.

From our earliest years we learn what will be approved and what will be rejected. Some children are rejected out of hand no matter what they do. Others are accepted if they conform. Most people spend their lives seeking approval. We all need to be loved and valued, but if we find (as most people do find) that who we are is not acceptable, then we distort ourselves to fit whatever it is that the person whose love we need will accept.

So most people are fashion-conscious. Others try to keep up with the Joneses. Christians try to be what other people insist is what a Christian should be. And what happens to the selves that God created? They go underground and we all become part of the faceless mass and we bore each other silly.

Let anyone step out of line and he is dubbed an eccentric, or a character, someone to smile about, to tolerate, to humour.

But there is no real line to step out of. Each of us is a unique, individual self, but instead of our being that, because we have experienced the withdrawal of love when we took our own line, we take a false line that was laid down, in the hope of being loved. And what do we get? One unreal human being, loving another unreal human being and we end up in total confusion about who we are and what love means. What a waste. What a betrayal of the marvellous creation that God himself created. He, God, created you and because you are afraid of being what he created, you try to be something that you are not.

Everyone I know is a 'con' man or woman to some extent. We present what other people want to see because we are desperate for love and approval. Sigmund Freud used to argue that civilized society needed this game of 'let's pretend'. He argued that civilization would blow up if we all expressed who we really are. I wonder? What he should have said was that if we expressed the pent-up fury that having to conform bred within us, then all hell would be let loose. But why is the fury there in the first place?

When Hitler was a youth, he failed to be accepted as a student by the School of Art in Vienna. He was also an unwanted baby. It all hurt him deeply. I believe that he had a choice. He could have accepted that rejection with dignity but he chose bitterness and diabolical, vengeful hate. What Hitler became, which for me was the incarnation of total evil, was the result of society's rejection and his choice to destroy. His future was made up of both elements.

It does not follow that a child with a perfect environment will become a perfect adult. The element of individual choice is always present. Thus a child born into a sin-sodden home can still choose the good, and a child born into a love-filled home can still choose the bad. But not many people swim against the tide either way.

One of the problems for children born into Christian homes is not knowing whether, if they themselves become Christian, it is because they are choosing of their own accord to be Christian. They have a fear that they are just reacting like robots to the input from their parents.

So here you are and maybe you have resisted all the attempts of parents, teachers, society, civilization, the Church and every other influencing agent that has an investment in forcing you to conform. You have fought the lot and you are standing on your own two feet, and the first reaction is to say, 'I am', followed pretty quickly by the thought, 'I am but I am alone'.

Existential Anxiety. We are now back to the title of this chapter. There you are, standing alone, fully aware that you are you, or in my case fully aware that I am me. We are no one's plaything. We have resisted every obvious and every subtle attempt to be taken over by the many agents that the devil has at his disposal to destroy our individual, God-created self.

But is there a God? You exist all right. I have no doubt at all about that. You may keep it well covered, but you are there and I am here. The question is, does the universe care?

You exist on a minor planet, belonging to an insignificant star (the sun) which is part of an insignificant galaxy in a universe that has millions and millions of galaxies much larger than the one that our star belongs to. And if our star burnt out it wouldn't be missed. You are one of billions of selves that have lived on this piddling little planet, which in itself is a piddling lump of matter that wouldn't be missed if it disappeared altogether. How can you be of any significance at all?

It is knowing that you do exist in a vast universe that would go on being the universe if you as you vanished without trace, that gives rise to what Paul Tillich called 'Existential Anxiety'. In other words, you know that you exist but it doesn't matter whether you do or you don't.

Earlier I spoke about people who lose their identity because they lose their job. Others lose their identity because they lose their wives or husbands. Others seek to find their identity by twisting themselves into a total mess, in order to fit into what society in this world (this insignificant planet, in this insignificant galaxy, etc., etc.) demands they should be.

But having faced all that and won through, you now stand alone and you ask the universe, with its billions and billions of stars, and trillions and trillions of planets, 'Do I matter, am I significant, does it matter what happens to me?' and the answer can come back, 'No! You are so insignificant that you are not as important as one grain of dust on the least significant planet of all the planets of the universe. You don't even live on a star, never mind living on a star that is an important star in a galaxy, and there are millions of galaxies much more important than yours.' That's how it feels for some people.

Shakespeare's Macbeth, for instance, saying that life 'is a tale told by an idiot, full of sound and fury, signifying nothing'. Again Shakespeare in 'The Tempest' has Prospero saying, as his conclusion to the question of life's meaning, 'Our revels are now ended, these our actors, as I foretold you, were all spirits, and are melted into air, into thin air; and, like the baseless fabric of this vision, the cloud-capped towers, the gorgeous palaces, the solemn temples, the great globe itself. Yea, all of which it inherit, shall dissolve, and like this insubstantial pageant faded, leave not a rack behind. We are such stuff as dreams are made on; and our little life is rounded with a sleep.'

Feeling *that* is what I understand Paul Tillich to have meant when he talked about 'Existential Anxiety'. The sheer naked terror of knowing that you exist, and yet in relation to the whole universe it doesn't matter a damn whether you exist or not.

I remember a Methodist preacher who was at the height of his powers in the late 1930s. His name was A. E. Whitham. I remember him saying that sometimes as he sat listening to a broken-hearted wife saying, 'My husband doesn't love me any more', he was asking himself the question, 'Does the universe love you, never mind your husband?' A terrible question.

Until you have stood there and asked *that* question you haven't even begun to understand what anxiety is really about. That anxiety grows from the knowledge of being able to say 'I am', but thinking that within the whole of this vast universe it doesn't matter whether I am or whether I am not.

Faced with this, the timid souls who have only glimpsed the power of that possibility run away from it, and refuse even to ask the question, 'Who am I?', because of the sheer terror of hearing the reply, 'You are nothing.'

There are a few brave people, many of them atheists, who ask the question, 'Who am I?', and accept the answer, 'You are nothing', but then go on to say, 'I will make the few years I have on this planet as tolerable as possible for myself and for other people'. These are the present-day stoics and I admire them. They ask the question, receive total rejection and then work to make life tolerable for as many people as they can. People who say and do that command my respect, even though I believe that they are wrong in their basic assumptions.

Do you now know what 'Existential Anxiety' is all about? If you do, what is your contribution to dealing with it? The way of the stoic? Or is there another way?

CHAPTER 10

Escapes from Loneliness

It is claimed today that the most terrifying experience that a small baby can suffer is to be left alone. For nine months the baby has been actually part of the mother. The baby's life has flowed from the mother. Food and oxygen have passed from the mother into the child.

It is also claimed that the process of birth can be a traumatic experience for the baby. The act of separation from the mother is experienced by all babies. The baby becomes separate.

Under clinically administered drugs many adults have re-lived their early weeks of life. Many have reported that what is called Separation Anxiety can be harmful.

There is no intention here of blaming mothers. In the course of a normal day a baby has to be left alone whilst the mother gets on with her work. A baby however has not got the intellectual equipment to understand that the mother cannot be there all the time. In those early days a baby has not had much experience of mother going away and then returning. Each departure of the mother could mean that she is going, never to return. In its helplessness, unable to get its own food, unable to protect itself, the baby feels the pain of utter loneliness.

During my travels in Africa I was fascinated to observe that the unsophisticated African mother did her day's work with the youngest baby strapped to her back. Could it be that these mothers, nearer to nature than we are, know instinctively that babies should never be left alone but should be in physical contact with the mother as much as possible?

If this thesis is correct then it follows that buried in the deepest memories of some of us lies the terror of having been left alone.

Loneliness then for most people is something to be avoided. For to be lonely now as adults can carry with it echoes of that original babyhood terror. I was talking yesterday to a young man aged 22 who was already feeling some panic that he might not meet a girl he could marry. At 22 afraid of future loneliness! I wonder how many marriages have been the panic-stricken result of this fear.

Alongside the baby's fear of loneliness there grows the feeling that a mother who can let you endure loneliness doesn't really care about you. She is someone not to be trusted. This does not imply that I am necessarily blaming the mother. It is simply an attempt to explain what is going on in the baby's mind. If that thesis is correct, then it also follows that because of that initial experience of feeling deserted no one must be trusted completely. It means that finally you may feel that even your closest friend is capable of deserting you.

So here we are on the horns of a dilemma. We need to be close to people in order to ward off the horrible feelings of loneliness, but we mustn't get too close in case we have to face again the dreadful feelings of desertion. We must not commit ourselves to anyone completely.

I have observed men whose wives have been unfaithful, or whom they have suspected of being unfaithful. Their feelings border on the murderous. They have trusted themselves to a woman and, like the child who has felt deserted by the mother, they feel helpless and the helplessness turns into destructive hate.

So we say, 'Please come close, but not too close'. Afraid to give ourselves completely in case we are let down, even the most balanced of us live on the fringe of loneliness, and prefer it.

This explains for me the phenomenon of the discotheque. You are in a crowded hall with a lot of people of your own age but the music is so loud that you cannot communicate verbally. Even modern dancing at 'discos' illustrates the point. You have a partner, but there is a three-foot gap between you.

Let us now look at another problem. I know that it is

stupid to generalize, but has there ever been an age when depression has isolated so many people? When depression has made every other human being appear threatening? What can be done about that?

You can, of course, retreat completely within yourself and ward off the horror of loneliness with drugs, drink or animal-like sex. Drink does change the personality. When talking with someone who has got plenty of alcohol working its way through the brain, you are not talking to the same person as when there is no alcohol affecting the same brain. I have had periods when I thought I needed alcohol. Friends have told me that with alcohol I change completely. I become very chatty. I go on and on, imagining that my conversation is fascinating, only to be told later that I had been totally and utterly boring.

Why do people drink? 'I go to the pub for company,' they say. Yet in an increasing number of pubs there is a 'group' playing, or there is taped music and it is so loud that you can't talk and be heard, and often it's not all that easy to think. I believe that alcohol creates the illusion that you are not alone, even though with it you are more lonely than ever.

What is depression? I cannot possibly claim to be an expert about it, but I have been treated for it. What is it? I've heard many explanations. All I can say is that for me it goes hand-in-hand with feeling cut off from the rest of mankind. When depressed I feel I am a total failure. I feel utterly unacceptable to the human race. I cannot be reached by love. Attempts made by people to care for me make me angry. I don't want to know and I don't want to be known. And it's hell. I am wrapped in a cocoon of misery.

Some drugs can lift the blackness, but they can be death-traps because their effect is only temporary, and you have to go on taking them, and as the body becomes resistant to them the dose has to increase and increase. You can become utterly dependent and the drug that is warding off the blackness and misery can slowly destroy you.

At the heart of depression is loneliness. Not being able to trust that you are really loved. The truly depressed person doesn't just look on the human race with suspicion, he doesn't really care if it ceases to exist altogether. He may commit suicide, which is the ultimate form of escape. Or he may turn to drink or drugs, which finally are just another form of suicide. Or he becomes hyper-active, giving himself no time to think. He lives permanently on the move.

Loneliness can result from anxiety. Not just ordinary commonplace worry. Ordinary worry can be shared and should be. Only a stupidly proud person refuses to share his worries. There is always someone to share them with. It could be a wife, a husband, a friend, the doctor, the clergyman. There is a wealth of deep human understanding waiting to share your burden if you will open your heart to another human being. The world is not full of moralistic people waiting for the chance to condemn you. On the contrary, most people, because they are aware of their own failures and anxieties, are able to listen to yours.

What bothers me are people who are so filled with anxiety that they have long since lost hope that anyone could understand. This kind of anxiety can best be described as panic. In this state the whole world is the enemy. If you have never known this condition in yourself, don't imagine that because you haven't known it, no one else has. What do you do when this kind of panic erupts? You can drink yourself silly and not care if you live or die or if anyone else lives or dies. But there is always the 'morning after' when the panic returns with increased power. You can cling to other people with the unspoken cry, 'Don't leave me, please don't leave me.' Yet leave you they must because they have their own lives to live and other responsibilities to face.

If you know how this panic feels, then please understand that I know that feeling and later on I will try to explain how I have managed to cope with it.

I have called this chapter 'Escapes from Loneliness'. There is alcohol. There are drugs. There is clinging to another human being. There is being hyper-active. There is sex.

In a way I suppose sex appears to be the best form of

escape. You can drink on your own and imagine that loneliness doesn't hurt. Drugs can give you the euphoric feeling that you love the whole human race, but you can be completely alone while you are feeling that. You can cling to another human being, but in your heart you know that they wish you would go away. You can be as busy as a bee helping and serving other human beings, but you know what you are doing. You are doing good not for someone else's sake but for your own. It is the subtlest form of trying to avoid loneliness that I know. It has all the marks of complete unselfishness, and yet it is probably the worst form of selfishness there is.

A girl who works in a factory told me the other day that she had problems at home. Before she came to see me she had been to the foreman of the shop floor where she worked. She went to see him and began by saying, 'Excuse me, but could you spare a minute to listen to the problems that I have at home?', and he said, 'Clear off [not his actual words!], I've got problems of my own'. That was honest. I actually know many 'do-gooders' who use their involvement in other people's problems to ease their own loneliness. I'm not saying that doing that is necessarily wrong. It can be salutary to care about someone else's problems that are far worse than your own. It puts your own into perspective. I went once to a hospital where children lay helpless because of brain damage. Looking at them made my own problems insignificant. Even so I am still prepared to say that caring for other people worse off than yourself can be used as an escape from your own isolation and loneliness. I am not saying that 'do-gooding' is wrong, but what I am saying is that if it is only an escape from loneliness, then to face the loneliness and win that struggle would make you an even better doer of good. You would not then be using other people apparently worse off than yourself to solve your own problem. I know that God can use our own brokenness to help other people. But it is not his will that you should remain broken. Jesus was broken on Calvary and through that he saved the world. But there was a resurrection for him. He didn't stay on the cross for ever and ever. Your brokenness can help others, but you don't have to remain broken. I am not saying that Jesus used our plight to solve his problem. What I am saying is that we can use other people's problems to try to solve ours. Jesus acted from strength to save the world. I am saying that we often act from weakness and use other people's needs to try and solve ours.

What about sex though? How much sex is about giving and not taking? I can't speak for women because I am a man. I suspect though that for women a lot of sex is answering the need to be wanted. I know about men because I am one. It can be animal. That is, release of a primitive urge. In animals it only happens as an instinctive drive to procreate. With man it can be just as animal, with no love present but with due precautions to make sure that there is no new birth as a result. That is sex in its lowest form. With a lot of men sex arises from the need to be close, to be intimate, to be one with another human being, to stave off loneliness.

I have been interested over the years to listen to what men say 'switches them on' about a woman. It may be her face, her mouth, her breasts, her bottom, her thighs, her legs, her ankles. Why can't it simply be her? Gilbert, of the Gilbert and Sullivan operas, had spotted this when he wrote the line for the Mikado's daughter who said that she 'had a lovely elbow'.

I don't know what women mean when they say that a man is 'dishy'. Do they mean that here is a man to whom they could relate? Or here is a man who could end their feelings of loneliness? If that is what they think, then I'm afraid they could be utterly disappointed if they won his interest. It is not easy for men to be interested in anyone but themselves.

I do understand the feeling that 'if only he knew me he would treasure me for ever'.

In 1945 Vera Lynn came to Karachi in India and sang in front of 5,000 men who hadn't spoken to an English girl for years. Although I was only one of the 5,000 I KNEW that she was singing only for me! On the way home I nearly had a fight with another serviceman who had the audacity to say that she had sung only for him. We both felt that if only she knew us she would fall for us.

We all have these fantasies, that the woman or man of our dreams would bring an end to the intolerable loneliness that we feel in our hearts. They don't exist. They are fantasies. All there is, are other people like you, loving sometimes, not loving at other times.

Sex, even with someone we really love, someone we really know, will not banish the basic loneliness we feel in our hearts. The answer to that lies somewhere else. Sex at its best can be nothing but good. For a while the loneliness can be banished, we can be one flesh. Jesus did say though that in heaven there would be neither male nor female, so he must have had something else in mind if what we are looking for is the end of loneliness.

I would like to end this chapter about escapes from loneliness by being personal. At the blackest period of my life, when I felt terribly lonely, I was completely and utterly tied to alcohol, believing that it would ease the pain. Those who know the problem that drink causes will know well the route that I followed. In 1964 an alcoholic drink was a rare experience in my life. By 1973 it had become a habit. It was all so easy. The drink at lunchtime whilst enjoying the respite from the ceaseless demands of my work. The drink after work before going home. One drink was soon not enough to get that 'feeling'. It had to be two pints of beer not one. Then it was two pints of beer and a whisky. For two years I didn't even notice that I had slipped into this routine. Then I faced the panic of needing a drink when it was unobtainable, and began to plan in secret that such an eventuality would not happen. At the time I believed that no one knew, that my secret was being well kept. What a fool I was. It is impossible to hide the fact that you are drinking, especially amongst those people who know you well. There came a desperate feeling of being trapped. You need the drink, but you feel so guilty and such a terrible failure because you cannot break the vicious circle that you are in. You drink to ease the guilt or the anxiety that drinking causes, and by doing that you only increase the guilt and the anxiety, so more drink is a necessity to ease that mounting guilt and anxiety.

It helps not at all for other people to berate you. You have sufficient self-condemnation without needing the condemnation of anyone else. Nothing can be done for you until you yourself reach the point where you are willing to acknowledge your dependency on drink. Before you reach that point there is a terrible period of loneliness, when you are trying to hide what you are doing from the people who would disapprove, and you seek out drinking companions who don't condemn you because they are in the same trap as you are. You imagine that these people are friends. But they are not. Kind and generous, yes, but they could never be called friends because you never meet them when you are sober. The whole of the relationship is built on what alcohol is doing to you both.

It took me at least three years after realizing that I was dependent on alcohol before I was able to struggle free. I am surprised, looking back, how little actual struggle there was to give it up, once I had acknowledged my dependency. To begin with it was hell. I had to sit clutching the arms of a chair, looking at my watch and counting the minutes till I knew that the off-licence was closed. When the urge came to go and get some alcohol I looked on it as a personal battle, and I called out to Jesus Christ to give me the strength to resist. There were times when he took the need for alcohol away and there was no problem, but then under strain the need would return. I slipped up several times, but each time I did I saw myself for the fool I was. I quite coldly examined what would happen once the alcohol had got into my brain. I may have been sitting alone feeling very anxious, and my mind would be saying, 'Go and get something to drink, that will ease the panic'. But my brain said, 'No it won't. It will fuddle your brain and the guilt afterwards for having failed will be enormous'. I had to choose between the anxiety or the guilt. I chose to face the anxiety soberly and prayerfully and to wait for it to ease of its own accord. Today the thought of what alcohol can do to me is enough to keep me away from it. For me it is poison.

We are obviously not all the same. Alcohol does not do the same thing for everyone. It may not be poison for some. He is a wise man who realizes that if it *is* poison for him, then it is quite simply that, poison.

There are alcoholics for whom the battle to stay clear of the stuff is a daily battle and always will be so. I wish them well in the battle. I know something of what it is like. But to those who have friends or relatives who are in alcohol's grip, a kindly word of advice. Your condemnation will not help. The person who helped me most was a kind and wise friend who said, almost off the cuff, 'If you are going to have a drink, then you might as well enjoy it'. That was the moment when I first saw a ray of hope that one day I would be free. Strange that, but true. I can hear echoes of the words of Jesus to the woman who was a slave to physical sex, 'I do not condemn you, but don't do it again'. It was in the refusal to condemn that she was helped to get off the hook.

Drugs haven't been my problem. I have no qualifications to speak to those for whom drugs are disastrous. But I have been to pot-smoking parties. That is an odd experience. Sitting with a group of, say, nine people having friendly conversation, everyone reasonably happy, and then the lit, pot-filled cigarette is handed round. Being the odd one out who didn't take his turn I was able to observe what happened to those who did. The idea was that as we were all in a friendly mood the 'pot' would make us even friendlier, and it would draw us even closer together. In fact the opposite happened. As the drug took effect, so each smoker seemed to distance himself from the rest, until instead of continuing to be a group we became isolated individuals. But only I knew that, because I alone was unaffected by the drug. The rest had the illusion of a growing nearness to one another, but that was quite clearly not the case. Alcohol and drugs have this in common, that either can be used, not only when there is panic, misery and despair, but also when people are comparatively happy, and the thought takes charge that the alcohol or drugs will increase the happiness and the friendliness. They do neither. In fact they destroy whatever true nearness and happiness is there, and offer only an illusion.

I am not a gambling man. Twenty pence on the Derby is about my lot. But I have friends who are addicted gamblers. There is Ron from Glasgow. Bliss for him is a pint of beer, the racing page from the newspaper, a friendly pub, and two hours before the 'off', time to make his calculations. For those two hours the world is a beautiful place in which to be. I met him when he was trying to get off his addiction. He was a lovely person when I met him. He told me that he wasn't a lovely person when all the races had ended and all his money gone. But why addiction to gambling? I have never found out. I have read that it can be a substitute for sex. That the final moment at the winning post is like an orgasm in sexual intercourse. That may be true. What I do know is that Ron never made it with his family. That he never got married. That he lived on his own. That to go back to his relatives would be to meet hard-faced rejection. I have been in casinos and observed the gamblers at work. Lonely people. Each absorbed in the 'wheel' and the little spinning ball, and their chips in the square of their choice. It is a lonely pastime, but carrying with it again the illusion that you are not alone because the place is crowded with people.

And what about radio and television? Having worked for the BBC for nine years and broadcast for them and Independent television and radio many, many times both before that period and after, I am not exactly in the 'knocking of broadcasting' game. I can however see that broadcasting is both a curse and a blessing. It is a commonplace now to say that television has destroyed the art of conversation. Just as common is the claim that television has made us a nation of watchers and not doers. We even had television laughing at itself in a series of programmes in 1977 saying, 'Why don't you *do* something instead of watching television?' Broadcasting is quite an extraordinary phenomenon. You sit alone in a radio studio and as far as your senses tell you, you are speaking only to yourself. There is no evidence that anyone at all is actually listening. Then there are listeners or viewers who imagine that the broadcast is happening only for them and for no one else. I know one broadcaster, who had a name known to millions, who told me that when she came on television one viewer had written to say that he poured out two glasses of sherry, one for him and the other he put on top of the television set for her! I have received countless letters from listeners and viewers who treat me as their closest friend, and yet I have never met them nor am I likely to. One broadcaster who worked for me ended what he had to say on the air with an invitation to anyone who felt that he could help them, to write to him. He received 1,600 letters and apart from six from cranks, all the others were genuine cries for help. What a terrible indictment of society that so many people turned for help to a disembodied voice. Was there no one nearby to whom they could turn? Apparently not. Or is it that to speak face to face with someone is more difficult than to write to someone who doesn't know you?

I am not underestimating at all the enormous benefits that broadcasting can offer. People who cannot sleep can at least listen to a friendly voice throughout the long, lonely nights. People who live on their own and who are unable to explore the riches of aloneness can receive some succour from the broadcast voice or face. Information that otherwise we would not have arrives in our living-room. Sometimes I feel that there is too much information to cope with. People who would love to go to church but cannot because of age, illness or household ties, can at least worship second-hand, which is better than not being able to worship at all. But by far the greatest danger of broadcasting is that we are tempted to get involved in unreal relationships with television personalities, or acted situations, and thus avoid the face-to-face encounter with people and with life. And spare a compassionate thought for the broadcasters. They too are in great danger. They can suffer from the illusion that they have countless friends because listeners and viewers appreciate the image that the radio voice, or the television picture, conjures up. One lady said to me, 'When I used to listen to you on the radio I used to long for the chance to meet you in the flesh. Now I have met you it has been such a crushing disappointment!' It was a good thing that I hadn't been 'conned' by my broadcasting popularity to imagine that it was actually me who was popular. The casualty rate of people, and marriages, and relationships amongst broadcasters is very high. In the 1930s there was a clergyman who broadcast every Wednesday evening. He was heard by millions, and his postbag contained thousands of letters every week. He ended up a lunatic in an asylum!

Very simply, and you have heard this many many times, let us see broadcasting for all the benefits that it offers, but let us never be unaware of its dangers.

So there we are. Loneliness that comes at us in many forms. Each of us in our own way trying to escape from it. I wonder if the way out of it is not to look for a way of escape at all, but to go right on into it, and from somewhere summon up the courage to face it? I know someone who did not run away, he found another way of dealing with it, and we have never forgotten him. His name is Jesus.

CHAPTER 11

Is Suicide the Answer?

'To be or not to be, that is the question,' said Hamlet. He said it when the demands of life had become too much and he was holding a knife (bodkin) pressed to his heart. 'Shall I kill myself or not?' he asked.

To be or not to be who you really are, I have already dealt with. To contemplate suicide or to do it is something else. I have had my fair share of people who have thought about doing it, or have attempted it, or have actually committed it.

What is suicide all about?

The attempt can mean two things. It can be a real attempt but someone steps in and the attempt fails. Or it can be an attempt in the hope that it won't succeed, but that it will be noticed. In this case the attempt is a cry for help or a threat.

'Norman' tried three times to commit suicide and each time, having taken enough tablets, rang me up from a phone box and told me what he had done. Each time I found him. Each time he became more difficult to find. Each time I rushed him to hospital and out came the stomach pump. I told him after the third time not to bother to ring me up the next time he did it, because I wouldn't bother to go and find him. He knew that I meant it and he hasn't tried since. What was he doing? His wife wasn't in love with him any more. In fact she didn't even want to live with him. His suicide attempts were simply those of a lonely man saying to his wife, 'Please don't leave me', and he was trying to squeeze out of her a love for him that she no longer had. When he finally faced the fact that she didn't want to live with him and accepted the pain which that caused him, he no longer threatened to kill himself.

Many attempts at suicide are a cry for help. 'I am desolate. I need love. I'll force you to love me.' What a comment on us when people have to attempt suicide in order to draw our attention to their plight.

But it isn't all that simple. A young man knocked on my door at one in the morning and asked if I could help him to get drugs. I had no access to drugs and no idea where they could be obtained. He said that if I didn't get them for him (at 1 a.m.!) then he would kill himself. I translated that as emotional blackmail, but I gave him a bed for the night and in the morning told him to go. He went, but as he went he said, 'You'll be sorry when they find my dead body'. I shrugged that off as another meaningless piece of emotional blackmail. Later on that day the police called and told me that they had just managed to grab him as he was jumping off London Bridge. He might have made sure that the police *would* grab him, but I couldn't be certain. I don't treat threats of suicide, or attempts at it, lightly any more.

What is the threat to commit suicide, or the attempt that is calculated not to succeed, all about?

It can be the desperate cry of a lonely person. It can be a cry to be noticed. It may be the cry of someone in terrible mental pain. It can be emotional blackmail aimed at forcing someone whom they want to want them. It is a very clever person who can sort out which is which. There is a commonly held idea that someone who says out loud that they are going to commit suicide doesn't really intend to. It is simply a warning saying, 'Do what I want or else you'll be sorry'. I think that is true in the majority of threats or attempts, but how can you be sure?

That theory however is supported by the shock one feels when someone who has given no sign at all that they are even contemplating it, actually does it. There was a man in the choir who lived alone, but in company was very sociable. A devout Christian who laughed a lot. He was found hanging from the banister at the end of a rope. What was the secret agony that he had successfully hidden for all those years?

There was a vicar, a predecessor of mine in a parish

where I was once vicar. He was found hanging from the bell-rope in his church tower. What had driven him to it? There was a Christian minister I knew well, married, with two daughters at college. He shot his brains out. Why?

Oh yes, it can happen to Christians, there is no point in hiding the fact.

All threats of suicides, all attempts at suicide that are planned not to succeed, and attempts that are planned to succeed but which are foiled, and all attempts that do succeed, have one thing in common. They all erupt out of loneliness. It is either 'I need love,' or, 'I need understanding,' or, 'No one does love me,' or, 'No one *could* love me'. They all spring from the soil of isolation, imagined maybe, but felt to be real.

But some attempts at suicides, and some actual suicides, cannot be explained that way. Almost always the coroner brings in the verdict: 'He took his own life while the balance of his mind was disturbed'. That has always rung a hollow note for me, because I haven't yet met the person whose mind isn't disturbed. That verdict makes it easier for the mourners. In spite of that verdict, however, which could cover most of our anti-social activities most of the time, I believe that for coroners to go on saying that is mixing up two vital issues.

We used to have a verdict, *Felo de se*, meaning 'he killed himself knowing what he was doing'. I believe that some people do that. Some people have the feeling that if the real truth were known about them, then rejection would be total. And people who cannot stand the isolation and loneliness that they feel and think would happen if the truth were known, end their lives. They feel that we couldn't be trusted to go on loving them when we knew the truth about them. A lot of actual suicides, I believe, come from that feeling. A man I know told me that since his brother committed suicide he had lived with a sense of guilt that couldn't be banished, and he told me that everyone who had a relative or close friend who had committed suicide would feel the same. Why? 'Because,' he said, 'you torture yourself with the thought that you could have done more. You could have been kinder and more understanding and more worthy of the suicidal person, who could have trusted in you.' Which says again that people who do commit suicide do it during a terrifying moment of feeling isolated and completely lonely, and that can be rational. That doesn't imply necessarily an unsound mind. It could simply imply a terrible judgement on us. Our love appears to be too frail to accept the self-loathing that the potentially suicidal person feels for himself. And could that not be true? How far would *your* love and acceptance go before it collapsed in the face of the horror and condemnation you might feel if you knew the deep secret truths about another human being?

Only one person can be totally trusted here. That person is Jesus. You may feel that there is no human being alive who could go on loving you and accepting you if all the truth about you were known. That could be true. But you just can't say that about Jesus. He is alive now. But on that cross where he was crucified he was taking upon himself the worst that you have ever done, the worst that you are now and saying, 'I don't condemn you, I accept you, my love can never be broken and what is more I will help you to become the person that in your heart you want to be'. It is there, and only there, that we can be saved from the overwhelming self-condemnation that could lead us to destroy ourselves. This is just one reason why the fact that Jesus is alive and that he loves us and that his love is unbreakable, must be made known.

Some people however attempt, and sometimes succeed in the attempt, to commit suicide because all that they want is to get revenge. Because you haven't loved me in the way I wanted you to, because you have rejected me when I needed acceptance, because in other words you will not be what I want you to be, then I will kill myself in the hope that you will feel the terrible guilt for my death for as long as you live. In other words, that is saying that I will only go on living if you are what I want you to be. The object of this whole book lies in the hope that you will never be driven to say that. Your well-being, your value as you, does not depend on what other people do or say. If you think it does, then I do not believe that you are of unsound mind. I think that that state of mind arises simply because you are too proud to admit that it is the love of Jesus that you need, or because no one has ever explained to you in a way that you can understand that he is alive and that he does love you. He is not there to be the Jesus that you want to force him to be (when he was on earth in the flesh people tried that one, but he wouldn't have it). He is with you all right, loving you and caring for you, not necessarily being the person you want him to be, but being himself and loving you as he is being that. He will not fit into the mould that you have made for him. You have to see him in his own selfhood and know that within that he is saying, 'I love you in yours'.

When I said that the coroner was mixing up two vital issues I meant it. There are people who commit suicide when their minds *are* sound, when they really do know what they are doing. What they are doing is mistaken and wrong but that is what they are choosing. I believe that they do it out of a feeling of terrible loneliness. That may be our fault but it may be theirs through refusing to face aloneness with Jesus. At one time no one who had committed suicide could be buried in consecrated ground. They were doomed because of what they had done. It is not for us to judge the rights and wrongs of that act. The blame could be theirs but it also could be ours. A judgement about that is much too complex for us. That judgement belongs only to God and because he is a God of love, real love, we should be content to leave the person who has committed suicide in his hands.

The coroner however is sometimes right when he says that a person has committed suicide whilst of unsound mind. Murder is often committed by people of unsound mind. In their defence they may say, 'I don't know why I did it'. That could be true. They may have been drunk at the time, and no one who has got alcohol inside them will think and behave as they would without it. Their minds are unsound. But without alcohol, we can still behave in ways that are unusual for us. I know this from personal experience. I have been so low at times that I have considered suicide as the only way to ease the pain of feeling a total failure. I have thought that the people I know and love would be better off with me out of the way. I didn't do it, because on the one hand it would have heaped guilt on to the people who loved me, and on the other because at the end of the day I am not a coward. Suicide, when I have felt like doing it, was a coward's way out. I may not be a hero but also I am not a complete coward.

However, I have known two occasions when suicide came near, not because I was choosing it, it was being chosen for me! By whom? I don't know. I remember vividly walking to where I keep medicines and taking the bottle of tablets for headaches and swallowing them all, one at a time. Fortunately there weren't enough to kill me. It wasn't 'Me' doing that. I was acting like a robot. Now that is really frightening. The thought that I could do something which I had no intention of doing scares me stiff, but it happened twice. Read St Paul, Romans chapter 7 verses 15 to 25 in the Bible. He did things that he didn't choose to do, but he still did them.

That is what being of unsound mind is all about, and it could happen to any of us. Not necessarily an attempt to commit suicide, but also in all sorts of other ways. Have you never said or heard someone else say, 'I don't know what came over me'? The psychiatrists would say that it is explained by some split off part of us that we will not acknowledge or accept about ourselves, taking over. All right, fine, good words, but useless. If there is a part of you that you can't accept, that you have split off, what alchemy is going to help you gather in the part or parts that you can't accept?

I am positive that it all boils down to the need for someone, somehow, to keep on relating to you. Split off bits of you may try to take over, but if you, the you that has some parts split off, is constantly being asked to affirm himself, then the split off bits have no chance of taking over.

Look at it this way. Suppose that Yehudi Menuhin,

the violinist, lost his arms in an accident, would he still be Yehudi Menuhin even though he couldn't play the violin any more? Of course he would. Mohammed Ali without his fists? The Beatles with no guitars? Jesus Christ when his whole body was dead? You may have split off your anger, or your compassion, or your violence, or your tenderness, but there is still you. The big question is, what is going to control your attitude to yourself and to other people? You, or a split-off bit of you? I am claiming that there is an irreducible you no matter how many bits are split off. It is the you that God made. You can be angry, you can love, you can feel foul, but it is you that is being all that and more. It is that you that Jesus loves. He loves you neither less nor more whether you are being loving or hating. What he wants and what I should want is that the me who I am should be able to fend off any split-off bits that may take control. The devil as an absolute being is evil. You as an absolute being are not evil. You are what God made and that is good. But experience of one kind or another may have encouraged you to jettison what truly you should be able to control, like anger, hate, love, kindness. The way to recover all the separated bits is for you to know that Jesus loves you and as you accept his love more and more, so the split-off bits come more and more under the control of you living in his love and then they can never take control of you again.

The coroner may be right sometimes when he says, 'He took his life whilst of unsound mind'. What I am saying is that he took his life when some split-off bit of him took over. Let Jesus love you and that could never happen.

When Hamlet said, 'To be or not to be?' he wasn't sure whether to be or not to be himself. He went on to ponder the thought that if he did kill himself then that would be the end of all his troubles, but then he had another thought. 'To die' yes, that would be all right, 'but perchance to dream'! Horror! Suppose death wasn't the end? Suppose that in killing himself he hadn't succeeded in killing his self but only his body?

And that is precisely what the Christian faith says. The

death of your body is not the end of you. Suicide is no escape. And it isn't. Neither is death from any other cause. Some people (bless them) wish it were. How can a loving God want me to go on feeling what I am feeling now for ever and for ever and for ever? The answer is that he doesn't. But if you choose to, then he will let you, because his love for you is such that he will not force you to choose what he wants, he allows you to do the choosing. I don't think that hell will be all that terrible for those who choose it. It will be what they have decided they want. No love, no being loved. No truth, only lies. No kindness, only viciousness. No peace, only violence. Is that what you want? The choice is yours. He has made the invitation into heaven possible. If you choose hell, then don't blame anyone else, it is your choice. The road to hell, said Jesus, is easy and anyone can choose it. The road to heaven is mighty tough and not many people choose it. But the choice is and for ever will be yours.

Jesus is there, with you now as you are reading this. He is saying, 'I love you'. You can accept that or turn it down. I hope with all my heart that whichever way you choose you will accept the responsibility that it is you who is making the choice. Don't fall into the dehumanized position of blaming someone else.

The choice is yours.

There is another thing that you can choose to do, and at first sight it seems so trivial. You can look up the phone number of the Samaritans in your area and ring them up. You may feel that you just have not got the faith to trust in a Jesus Christ that you cannot see. Could you trust that at the end of the telephone, if you ring the Samaritans, there is someone you could talk to who would not run away? They could not give you faith in Jesus Christ, who is the ultimate answer to the loneliness that drives one to thoughts of suicide, that is something that only you can have, no one can give that to you, but it has helped countless people to be able to talk to another human being about the deep blackness and despair that life can bring. I have worked for the Samaritans and also know of their work in other areas. The connection cannot be proved but there is no doubt that since the Samaritans were formed the rate of suicide has decreased.

Finally, though, we can only rest in total security when we rest in the love of Jesus Christ, but meanwhile, the number of your local branch of the Samaritans isn't difficult to find, and even if the rest of the world doesn't want to know how you are feeling, they do.

CHAPTER 12

Who Was He?

I thought of heading this chapter with the title of 'Who was Jesus?' Then I thought of someone seeing this book in a shop and picking it up, and seeing the name of Jesus perhaps quickly putting it down thinking, 'That's about religion and I'm not religious'.

Nor am I in the sense that religion can be both boring and irrelevant. I hesitate sometimes to tell people that I love Jesus because of all that they might think I mean when I say it.

There is no doubt at all for me that Jesus lived. I get bored or irritated by people who can quite easily accept the idea that Julius Caesar lived, and that the Romans lived in Britain before Jesus was born, but then try to persuade me that no such person as Jesus ever lived. That is simply rubbish.

I believe that I have the right to say (because I have done a lot of work to find out) that Jesus did actually live. There is vastly more evidence that Jesus lived than there is that Julius Caesar lived.

Either you trust the historical evidence that supports the proposition that Jesus lived and that the record of his life in the New Testament is true, or you do not. I trust the records.

He was a very mysterious person. He was truly a man. He worked as a carpenter. He came from a relatively poor home. He knew what hunger was like. He knew thirst. He enjoyed parties. Women loved him and so did men. Hard, tough men counted it a privilege to be called his friends. Prostitutes didn't run away and hide when they knew he was about. They knew that he was a man but they also knew that he wasn't interested in buying their bodies. Lonely people felt accepted by him. Sick people tried to get near him. Lunatics found that he understood them. Children were happy with him. There were of course people who wanted to use him for their own ends. Some of them wanted an Oliver Cromwell kind of figure. Some probably wanted a Hitler kind of figure, provided he supported their cause. I've even heard people liken him to Lenin. He was none of these. He was always and only his own man.

But there was something about him that they couldn't explain. The people who knew him best said that he was a man all right but there was something else, something about him that they trembled to say. It was obvious to the people who knew him best that he was truly a man, but how could they explain the 'other' that they knew he was? Eventually all they could say was that Jesus was God.

I have known several people who have thought that they were God. I don't mean people who act in a bossy way and you say, 'He thinks he's God, he does'. I mean people who because they were mentally deranged imagined that they were God. Jesus never said that he was God in that way. It was other people who said this about him. It was the only way that they could describe what they felt when they were with him. They saw him as a man. They knew that he knew what it was like to be hungry. They watched him cry when a friend died. They saw him when he was tired. They saw him being angry. They saw a man. But they saw something else! There was something about this man that couldn't be explained in human terms. The only way that they could explain him to themselves was by saying that Jesus was a man but also God. Not just any old god, he was THE God.

It is mind-boggling to think that thought: that this man was the God of the whole universe. This man whom they could touch, see and smell was the God of all creation. It doesn't make any kind of sense. I believe that the people who knew him best were honest reporters. If he had only been a tremendously great human being then that is what they would have recorded.

There was a Roman Emperor called Caligula who thought he was a god and who made his horse a Senator (like being a member of the House of Lords), and the people around Caligula pretended to believe that he was a god. They didn't really believe it, because they knew that Caligula was mad, but they pretended to because they were afraid of what he would do to them if they denied it.

Jesus did not go about saying, 'I am God, I am God, believe it or else'. He simply went about being himself and it was other people who said that he wasn't just a man. The only way that they could describe Jesus was to say that he was man and he was also God.

Take it or leave it. The people who knew him best said that he was both.

When I read what they wrote I feel exactly what they felt. I don't think that they were 'cooking the books'. After all, what was there in it for them? To be known as a Christian then was to risk being killed for even saying that Jesus might have been God.

I can find no rational reason for denying that Jesus was in fact God. I can't understand it. I don't know how it could have happened. All I know is that it did happen.

Even more difficult to understand is that the Jesus that they knew is alive now. The resurrection did take place. All kinds of people have tried to explain that it didn't happen, that it couldn't have happened, that there is no rational explanation of how it could have happened.

Again I have to repeat that the people who knew him best said that it did happen. Why should they proclaim as truth something that they knew was a lie? People who claim that what they said was not true fail to evaluate the power of the instinct for self-preservation. I have heard it argued that people have been willing to die for the belief that Communism or Nazism or some other creed was the truth. In a way I admire them. Anyone who is willing to give their own life for something that they believe is true must command some respect, no matter how wrong their belief may be. Few people give their lives away easily.

The men and women who witnessed the resurrection weren't willing to die for something that they believed was true, they were willing to die for what they knew was true.

Lots of people gave their lives afterwards for what they believed was true about Jesus, but it all began with a bunch of people who didn't just believe, they knew.

So, here was God who became man. This man called Jesus knew all about being human and because he was also God then I think he is worth listening to.

The records show that he was his own man. He didn't act out for his own parents. He didn't act out for his own brothers. He didn't act out for his friends. He didn't act out for his enemies. He was his own man. He was an 'inner directed' man. An 'inner directed' Hitler slaughtered six million Jews. An 'inner directed' you might do something monstrous, because we, and people like Hitler, have all kinds of pent-up feelings within us – frustration, repressed anger, incredible fantasies. Again as Freud said, to let the lid come off all that would lead to chaos. We need the checks and balances of lawful society to keep us in control. We all have it within us to smash, destroy and murder. We can't give vent to all our inner feelings. We are what the theologians call fallen people. There's hardly one saint amongst us. Left free with no outside restraints, the mind reels at the thought of what might happen.

In Jesus, the record says, there was no evil. Temptation yes, falling to temptation, no.

He belonged to the human race but he was not part of the world's fallen nature. He was unique. That is what I am asking you to believe when I invite you to become a Christian. I invite you to believe that Jesus, who shared your humanity and in whom you can find a friend, is also divine and able to lift you out of the morass that being human plunges you into. If he was only divine he would be too far away for us to reach. If he was only human then he could share the mess we are in but be unable to do anything about it. He had to be both. He was and is both.

Why did they crucify him? When you look at it closely I think it is clear why the people concerned did what they did. It was a soldier who hammered the nails through his hands and feet. Jesus didn't blame the soldier who did it or the other soldiers who were helping him. We are all guilty of saying that 'they' know best. We all need a 'they' to tell us what to do, to fix the rules, to make things work. We are so frightened and feel so powerless that we must have a 'Big Brother' who knows best.

I served for five and a half years in the RAF in the war. I did nothing glorious or courageous. I just did what I was told, in the innocent belief that 'they' who were in charge knew what they were doing. I did have a few moments of doubt, though. I remember when 'they' decided to send 1,000 bombers to blast Cologne to bits. I was working on an RAF station where we had six Wellington bomber aircraft. They had to be part of the 1,000 bombers which were destined for Cologne. Most of us knew that our poor, tired out Wellingtons would be lucky to reach the Channel, never mind get to Cologne and then get back. But eventually we settled for the idea that 'they' knew best. In the event, however, 'they' were proved wrong.

Since the war I have met personally some top politicians and top RAF and Army people. I know now that they were and are just human like the rest of us. They weren't supermen, just ordinary men with heavy responsibilities. 'They' don't always know what is best.

It all goes to show what folly it is to put our trust in 'top' people as though they were supermen. We all do it. We all think that 'they' know best. We all cling to the wish to have a 'daddy' because we are afraid of standing alone. So a few unknown Roman soldiers crucified the most wonderful person the world has ever known, because 'they' said it was the best thing to do.

The Roman soldiers crucified Jesus, but the 'religious' leaders arranged it. 'Religion' – what horrors it has caused. People seek status, power, and in the past wealth, all in the name of 'religion'. There are some men who I believe have refused to be religious leaders because they wouldn't play the 'religion game'. Others, good men, have accepted the role hoping that they wouldn't be corrupted by it. Some may have succeeded. I don't despise those who play the 'religion game' in order to get to the top of it. If I had been offered a top religious job I would most likely have accepted it and produced a thousand good reasons for doing so.

However, it was the 'religious' leaders who cried out for the death of Jesus. He was upsetting their apple cart by revealing the truth and by explaining what God is really about. If you are using God or religion to protect you from the truth about yourself and your own personal life, then you must treat as an enemy someone who is pulling the carpet from under your feet. Religion must not be used to protect you from the truth about yourself. Who are you? A religious leader? Someone respected by society? Someone who has power? Someone to whom other people defer? You are none of these things. You may be just another lost lonely soul like many of us, but it must be disturbing to have it pointed out.

What about the rest of us who aren't soldiers obeying commands, or leaders of 'religion' who have an investment in keeping 'religion' going? Why did we want Jesus crucified? We did you know. It was people just like us who wanted him out of the way. We felt safe within an untroubled world. We didn't really mind the Romans looking after us. We could tolerate the bishops and other church leaders so long as they allowed us to play our own games of make-believe. Along comes Jesus to ask you to be true to yourself. Not true to all those buried, destructive passions within you, but true to the you that God created. You sold that 'you' a long time ago in order to buy off the wrath and rejection that would fall on you if ever you were that. But there was a man called Jesus who said, 'I love you', not the you that is the result of fitting in with what society and religion demands. He loves you. The world doesn't want that you. A long time ago you learned that the world doesn't want that. The world is 'make-believe' and it wants you to be a 'make-believe' person. Deep down inside you don't want to be that. You want to be the you that God made, but if you become that then the world will reject you. So what do you do with Jesus who invites you to be the you that God made and says, 'I love you'? There is a choice. Either you kill him and keep your unreality intact or you will love him, become true, and probably get smashed to pieces by the world for not playing the right 'game'.

Jesus invites you to stand alone. He doesn't ask you to be lonely. He simply says, 'God created you, come with me and be who you are and discard these silly "games" of wanting and then trying to be what you are not'.

CHAPTER 13

More About Him

No one could accuse Jesus of being a lonely person. There is no hint that he ever said (even on the cross), 'No one loves me, poor old me'. His problem was that he was too popular. From when he was thirty there were always too many people around who wanted to touch him, or be touched by him, or talk with him.

He was the 'honoured guest' at fashionable parties. The 'common people' couldn't leave him alone. He was always in demand. The people nearest to him gave up all their security to be with him. In this man we are not seeing someone who craved human friendship because he was afraid to be alone. He related to whoever he met – the rich capitalist or the outcast leper, he could relate to them all, and until the end they all wanted to relate to him.

This was not a lonely man. Yet he needed to be alone.

Read Mark chapter one verse 35. He had worked all day and well into the evening healing people from the various ills that were crippling them. Which of us wouldn't have gone on an 'ego-trip' after being able to do that, wallowing in all the praise and glory? Not he. He cleared off in order to be alone.

There was the lunatic who had defied all attempts to keep him in check. Jesus brought him back to sanity and then what did Jesus do? He got into a boat and left the scene (Mark 5 verse 18).

He fed 5,000 people, who must all have been amazed at what he had done. What did he do next? Stay around to receive their adulation? No. He went off on his own to pray (Mark 6 verse 46).

Jesus was his own man. He spent a lot of time alone. He went into the wilderness alone after he discovered who he was. He went into the wilderness deliberately in order to work out what was involved in being himself.

He wasn't afraid of being alone. In fact the opposite was true: he had to be on his own at times in order to be true to who he was. There were so many people who wanted him to be what they wanted him to be. They pressed him to be a political leader, and to lead the partisans like Marshal Tito did in Yugoslavia. They wanted him to spend all his time being a healer like . . . well, I don't know who he could have been like. We have so many so-called 'healers' around these days. His mother wanted him to go back home and be 'normal'. His closest friends wanted him to destroy his enemies. A so-called king wanted him to do magical tricks so that he, the king, could be entertained. The religious leaders wanted him to do something that would prove that he knew, really knew, what life was about. What a joke! Even if he had done what they had asked for, they would still have murdered him. Their investment in the *status quo* was so total that they had no intention whatsoever of listening to what he really had to say.

In the event he didn't fall for any of the traps that people laid for him to be what they wanted. Quietly and with complete dignity he just went on being who he was, Jesus.

The nearest he came to loneliness, apart from on the cross, was in the Garden of Gethsemane, the night before he was murdered.

He had spent the evening with his friends. After supper he took them to a garden just outside Jerusalem. He knew that his enemies were planning to kill him. He also knew that there was no escape. I do not mean that he could not have run away. That would have been easy. He could not escape from the confrontation between what he knew life was about, and what others thought, or had persuaded themselves to believe, that it was about.

He knew he was going to be killed.

He asked his friends to go with him to the garden while he summoned up the courage to face what lay ahead. They went with him. But when it mattered most that they should support him, they fell asleep.

Alone, totally alone, he wrestled with what God, the God of the universe, was asking of him. As a man he retreated from the idea of being totally rejected. As a man he also accepted that if being a man meant facing what his enemies were planning, then he couldn't retreat, he had to go forward and go forward alone.

Lots of people have been rejected, some have even died rather than renounce their integrity. Martin Luther said, 'Here I stand, I can do no other'. Thomas à Becket died for what he believed was the truth. Joan of Arc did the same. There are hosts of others who have followed that path.

Has anyone else chosen death because he or she knew that to die could liberate the whole of mankind from a betrayal of their true humanity? That was what Jesus was struggling for in the Garden of Gethsemane. And he was alone. Many wonderful human beings have died for a truth and we praise them for what they did. Jesus chose to die so that all people for all time could be free to be what God had created them to be. If he had ratted in the Garden of Gethsemane, because he was man *and* God, then you and I, with the promise within us of being of infinite value within the whole of creation, would have been doomed. That is what he was fighting for. He fought there for you. So that you would know that being you was of infinite value. We throw away all the time what it was for which he fought and won in that garden.

The really big aloneness though was still to come. His enemies demanded his death. All people who are afraid to face the truth about themselves demand his death. 'Our' wish was granted. At all costs I mustn't face the truth about me. Yet, without us asking him to do it, he took our guilt for failure to be what God made us to be, all our lies, deception, cowardice and failure, on to himself and instead of leaving us to be destroyed because of what we have done, he allowed us to destroy him. And went on doing it as we drove the nails into his hands and feet. He did all that in the hope that we would accept his sacrifice so that we could be free to be what God created us to be.

On the cross, whilst he was going through all that,

something even more terrible happened. He had done what he did because he believed that through what he was doing God was rescuing us from the mess we are in. At the moment when he thought he had won, he felt that God himself had deserted him.

Could anyone ever again experience the depth of aloneness that he must have felt then? His closest friends had deserted him. His family thought that he was mad. He had one comfort left. God, to whom he belonged, would understand and stay with him. At the moment of his most extreme desolation he felt separated from God. How could this be? He *was* God. Yet God had left him. That is the ultimate of isolation, aloneness and rejection. You don't understand? Nor do I.

I can't explain what was going on at that moment on the cross. Only he knows that.

What I know is that there was no cry to be released from that agony. He was saying to God, who is the final meaning of the universe, 'Even though you desert me, I will be true to who I am for the sake of mankind'.

That is the final statement of your worth, your value. Jesus had become a man to show us just that. And God accepted that statement. In Jesus, man has shown what man can be. In Jesus, God has shown what he wants man to be, because God did it himself in Jesus. And God has shown what God is: someone who loves us so much that he would go through all that for us. All your sin, all your deception, all your lies, are nailed once and for all upon that cross. God says, 'I forgive the lot, now come and be who I created you to be'.

What a relief, what a wonderful relief. I don't have to creep about pleasing this one or that one. I can be the person that God created. I don't have to wallow in loneliness trying to 'con' you in order to please you.

I accept my 'aloneness' because I am someone whom God loves. Beneath all the nonsense that I present to the world as 'me', there is a real me and God himself loves and cherishes that.

Chapter 14

I Met Him

I was 15 at the time. Just the right time for a religious experience, so the cynics would say. I am a cynic, but listen to what happened.

I was used to going to church. My parents (God bless them) created a home where going to church was quite normal. I loathed it. Church services, and especially the sermons, bored me stiff. I had heard hundreds of sermons and sung hymns on thousands of occasions, and none of it connected with what my life was about. None of it connected with my passion for cricket and football, the cinema, or my growing interest in girls. The preachers were in a world of their own. They certainly didn't sound as though they knew anything about the world that I lived in.

Until that one night! The preacher wasn't even a 'Reverend'. He was a layman called Eddie Horton. That night he said, 'Jesus loves you'. He must have said lots of other things, but that's the bit I remembered. Jesus loves me? I suddenly felt a tremendous need to know if that was true.

As was our custom as a family, we all went home, each to do their own 'thing'. My mum and dad to listen to the radio broadcast from St Martin-in-the-Fields. My sister to do whatever she did in those days, and my brother to do his 'thing'. Mine could have been playing with my Meccano set. I sat around for a while, and then without telling any of them what I was doing I walked out of the house, towards the lane that led to a small grassy hill. I went out to look for Jesus. I did. I know it sounds mad but that is what I was doing. I got to the top of the hill. It was a dark night, no moon. I was alone. 'Where are you, Jesus?' I asked.

He was there. Quite simply there. I knelt down in the grass. It was muddy. What happened then is beyond the power of my words to describe. I knew that he knew me. I knew that he loved me. It wasn't sentimental. I didn't cry with relief. I was aware of a tremendous joy. I felt accepted, liberated, free.

I don't know for how long he was with me. All I know is that he was with me and then he went away. I knew he had been with me because when he went away there was an absence! He hadn't 'gone' in the sense that he ceased to exist. He had only gone in the sense of an actual personal encounter. He was still alive. I knew that he was still there but not in the vivid way he had been as I knelt before him.

'Of course, you were simply deluded,' some people would say. What they must not say is that I am lying. I am writing this with total honesty. Was I deluded? Was I projecting a deep passionate desire for someone to know me and love me?

I'm no fool. I am by nature a sceptic. I do not believe in mediums, seances, astral bodies, hauntings, ghosts and the like. I believe that astrology is bunk. I am the last person in the world to believe anything unless there is hard, unshakeable evidence. I am like St Thomas who couldn't believe that Jesus had risen from the dead until he saw the actual wounds in the hands of the risen Jesus.

Part of my reason for being psycho-analysed in my twenties was to find out if that experience of the presence of Jesus was only a delusion. Was it just me creating the answer to my own need? We are all capable of believing what we want or need to believe. Was I the victim of my own desire? The answer is that if I was, then psycho-analysis did not reveal that to be the case.

The years passed. I lived knowing that Jesus was alive. Never there in that immediate sense, although I asked and asked for him to be so. In times of utter dejection, depression and near madness I have pleaded for another 'visitation'. He never answered my need in the way I wanted it. I know that he is alive, I know that he is there, but he is not there like a drug to give me a boost when I feel utterly low.

He is there all right. I have never been able to forget it. He is there with forgiveness, understanding and strength. I live and keep going on because I know that.

I did 'meet' him again, but this time it wasn't in answer to my need. It was 1969. I was working for the BBC and they asked me to go to Jerusalem and with a tape recorder describe my thoughts and feelings at all the holy places.

It was a Thursday night. (I didn't realize it was Thursday night at the time.) It was 10 p.m. I was sitting in my hotel room listening to the recordings that I had made that day. For no rational reason I decided to go to the Garden of Gethsemane there and then. (It was on a Thursday night that Jesus went there for the last time, but I wasn't thinking about that at the time.) I left the room, and as I was walking out of the hotel the manager asked me where I was going. I told him. 'You won't get in at this time of night, but if you wait till the morning I will arrange for you to get in. They lock the gate at night,' he said. I thanked him and left the hotel. Gethsemane wasn't far away. Before I got there I had the idea of climbing over the wall if the gate was indeed locked. Not a hope. The walls around the garden were much too high to climb over. I arrived at the gate. It was very securely locked. I carried on walking round the wall. Eventually I had to walk up a dark track in order to continue following the wall. I was frightened. There could easily have been a terrorist or a 'mugger' hiding in the dark, waiting for some idiot like me. Then I came to a spot where the wall was being rebuilt. The workmen had knocked down a part of the wall and all I had to do was clamber over a pile of rubble to get into the garden.

I remember feeling like a thief. I had no right to go into that garden without permission. I am not by nature a law-breaker. I went in. In the dark the garden looked small. There didn't seem to be any grass. There were some trees, olive trees I supposed (after all, it was on the Mount of Olives). I tried to imagine where Jesus would have knelt that night he struggled with his Father to avoid the crucifixion.

I chose a spot right opposite where the gate in the wall of Jerusalem would have been when Jesus entered the city in triumph. I sat down on the soil. Jerusalem looked breathtakingly beautiful. The dome of the Mosque there was floodlit and the gold of the dome shone brightly. Cars drove past on the road outside the garden.

I began to think about Jesus. What was going on in his mind all those years ago when he had been in that garden on that night? And then he came! Again I repeat, I am not a fool. I know the difference between thinking about someone and actually being confronted by them. They are completely different experiences. He was there.

'What then,' I asked, 'was your struggle in this garden all about?' He told me, 'It was about being true to myself.' He said, 'A lot of me wanted to run away from what was going to happen.' I just can't write about the rest. It is all there inside me but for reasons that I can't understand I mustn't touch with my pen the full content of what happened.

What I can say is that he accepted who he was. That he chose to be himself. He was the Saviour. It was in his power to offer the salvation of freedom to every human being and no matter what the cost he was going to offer it. And that is exactly what he did.

And me? What did that encounter do for me? I left that garden that night knowing that there was only one way for me to go, and that was to follow my own integrity, to be true to the self that God had created me to be.

I haven't succeeded. I have failed a thousand times. I have sought praise and acted to get it. I have been false for fear of being rejected. I have sinned and kept it secret. I have pretended to love when I haven't felt loving.

I know, though, where life is. I know the pathway to the truth. I know that human life can have eternal significance. I know that every human being is of infinite worth. I know that within this vast universe there is the love of a God who is personal. That the meaning of the whole of creation is about love. I don't believe these things to be true, I know that they are.

I have only travelled a very short distance along the

road. It is up to others, more courageous and loving than I am, to go further.

Finally though I have to admit that when I say that I know that there is God and that God is love it isn't knowledge in the sense that I can communicate it. It isn't objective knowledge. It cannot be demonstrated. I have experienced three times a vivid sense of the presence of Jesus. I believe that they were genuine experiences.

> 'Lord I believe that you are there.
> Forgive me when the darkness comes
> and my faith begins to waver.'

CHAPTER 15

Loneliness — Aloneness

I think that all feelings of loneliness are bad. Either you shouldn't be in a situation where you can feel lonely, or you haven't solved the problem of being alone without feeling lonely.

Take the first of those. A lot of people who feel desperately lonely are feeling that on account of the sheer selfish, unimaginative attitudes of other people. Between now and when you are able to be alone without feeling lonely, a lot of people who could help have got to be alerted to what they could do.

I said earlier that a lot of elderly people are 'blood-sucking leeches', drawing the life-blood out of their children or 'friends'. I hold to that. I do not withdraw it. Such elderly people need to be made aware of what they are doing. However there are other elderly people who wouldn't dream of asking for help, and those of us who are younger should, out of our sensitivity, provide companionship without being blackmailed into it or being asked to provide it.

I am thinking of one old lady of 79 who lives entirely alone, whose son lives only a few minutes away from her, but rarely calls to see her. Maybe she was hopeless as a mother. Maybe he has got reason to feel hate and vengefulness for her. But there is such a thing as forgiveness even when it isn't deserved. She never asks her son to call.

There are people who live in loneliness who have not even deserved it. Some elderly people have been good and loving parents but are separated from their grown-up children by distance. Some of these people would not ask for help, their self-respect prohibits that (and God bless them for it, I say). To be offered companionship that hasn't been asked for might be welcome. Why not try it?

There are women and men who for one reason or another never got married. Some chose not to marry and their choice was clean and strong, and in my experience of them they carry on through youth, middle age and old age and never feel in the least dependent and do not sit alone in a sentimental mish-mash of 'nobody loves me'. I admire them. They have learned something of what aloneness is about and how wonderful it can be.

My heart goes out to those who desperately wanted to get married or who really want deep and fulfilling relationships but who have a block against achieving them.

I feel angry with whoever was responsible for the damage that caused such people to feel as they do. But to go out towards another human being does require courage, and there are some people who excuse themselves for not doing it by blaming someone in their past for not being able to do so. I would say to those what Cassius said to Brutus in Shakespeare's 'Julius Caesar', 'The fault, dear Brutus, is not in our stars, but in ourselves, that we are underlings.'

Freud has given so many of us so many excuses for avoiding the realization that it was and is our lack of courage or 'nerve' that we are what we are. It is so much easier to blame someone else for not having the courage to have a go. Other people did damage us, but the other people were themselves damaged by other people who were also damaged by other people and so on and so on until you get back to the Book of Genesis and Adam, who himself blamed Eve!

Of course there is a case to be made out for the effect that other people have on us. But it isn't a complete case. I believe that at the heart of every human being there is the ability to choose. I don't care what pressures from outside may be brought to bear, that ability to choose is always there. There may not be the slightest hope that the choice may be exercised, but the choice is there. You could argue that with modern methods of interrogation a human being's freedom to choose can be destroyed. I do not believe it. What I do believe is that most of us would renounce our freedom to speak and act freely at the first sign of suffering incurred for what we believed to be the truth.

I would have been a hopeless secret service agent. At the first sight of the pincers approaching one of my fingers to tear out the finger nail, I would have confessed to every secret I knew. I believe, though, that there are other people who would survive every kind of torture and would still refuse to divulge what they chose to keep secret.

There are people who believe that human beings are simply a conglomeration of chemicals, and that the introduction of the right chemicals at the right time could change any human being into what the operator chose. This I don't believe.

This method could succeed in 999 cases out of every thousand. I retain the belief that we are not only chemically structured, or electrically structured (if you think of the human being as simply a magnificent computer).

Right deep down in me there is me. Alcohol may make me think or do what is stupid. Even when that has happened I have known that it was me being stupid. Unless you make me unconscious then I do know what is going on, even though I may not exercise the freedom that I know I possess. There is no chemical (i.e. drug) that can take that away altogether.

I believe that this will be the great debate of the future. Genetic Engineering is the 'in' phrase at the moment. Aldous Huxley in *Brave New World* prophesied this possibility. He suggested that it was possible that man could create human beings to order. And so we might. Ten million people who are conditioned to accept that mining salt is what they wanted most of all to do. Another ten million people breaking rocks with hammers and accepting it without protest. Another ten million people working as slave labour doing whatever 'Big Brother' (who will also have been manufactured) decides is essential.

I believe that all that kind of thing could happen. Except that somehow, somewhere there would be one self who would say no! He or she would, with tremendous courage, keep their identity as a self intact. I believe that mankind is now at a crossroads. The forces at work to reduce us to robots reacting to any given stimuli are manifold. If you believe that there is no self within you that exists within its own right, then you will go along with what is already happening. Already we are being conditioned by powerful advertising. We are conditioned by the retention of class structures. Conditioned by the education we received, and allow our children to be given. The attitude of 'they know best' is like a cancer growing across our planet. 'They' may know best, but on the other hand, they may not. It may be true that we are simply the product of what input we have received, in which case we are simply the accidents of how a purposeless universe works, or a universe whose purpose is evil.

You have to choose. I trust the deep awareness that I am me. Conditioned, yes. Most of my choices could be predicted by someone who knows all the input that I have received. I said 'most'. I know that at the end of the day I am not that. I may go along with it because it is easy and it helps me to fit in with what society requires. But I know that within me there is a me and if I acquiesce with what the world is demanding then it is I who am acquiescing. But it could be me saying no.

Jesus had every conceivable reason for not being himself. He could have stayed at home and been a reasonably successful carpenter. Married. Some children. A few close friends and lots of acquaintances. A reasonably happy life. Or when he realized that he had a strange kind of power to command the attention of lots of people by his words and actions, he could have been persuaded to be a political leader. He might even have stepped on to the ladder of ecclesiastical power, even though the wrong party was in power at the time. The name of that game is 'wait until your lot come into power'.

You have to ask, 'What did he choose?' What his parents wanted? What his relatives wanted? What political leaders wanted? What ecclesiastical pundits wanted? What the common people (you and me) wanted?

He responded to none of these pressures. And when

Pilate (the Roman Governor of Jerusalem where Jesus was held captive) said that he (Pilate) had the power to release him and set him free, Jesus said, 'You have no power over me at all'. I love that.

Jesus was his own man. Even on the cross he chose when to die. Now, there's a mind-blowing thought. If the reporters got it right, and I believe that they did, he chose the moment when he would die. Matthew 27 verse 50: 'And Jesus cried again with a loud voice and released his spirit.' No one took his life from him, he gave it.

If you ever get the chance to see Salvador Dali's picture of the Crucifixion, or a copy of it, look closely, for you will see that there are no nails holding Jesus to the Cross. He was choosing to be there.

If he couldn't choose that, then for me no man or woman can choose anything, we are all the victims of what other people have done to us, or are doing to us now.

There are so many parents who imagine that they can condition their children to be exactly what they want them to be. Jesus's mother tried. Parents who try to do this may succeed, and in succeeding could destroy the self for which together they provided a body. Other parents will be affronted, disturbed or upset because their child has not lived out what they had decided he or she should be. The mother of Jesus wanted her son to be what she wanted. Her wish wasn't granted. Instead Jesus became his own man, and probably at the end she loved him more deeply because he had resisted her demands.

To me it seems obvious. I must be me. You must be you. As I said earlier, not become what our conditioning has encouraged us to become. Not be moulded by my frustration into a bitter, angry, resentful, suspicious, or even docile kind of person. My *raison d'être* is to be me and to fight with all my power to ward off the power of the outside world to manipulate me into being what they would prefer.

This does not mean that parents, teachers or authoritative people should not be an example. To be an example is to offer someone the chance to choose. But any attempt to condition that choice by emotional blackmail, be it threat or blandishment, I believe is evil. Point out the consequences either way by all means, but for anyone to say, 'I chose your way because you wanted me to choose it', is terrible. Of course I want them to choose my way, but they mustn't choose my way because that way is mine, they must choose it because it is theirs.

The result of other people not being what I want them to be is loneliness. Aloneness is when I can stand alone, no matter what other people say, or do or think. It is a hard road, or as Jesus said, 'It is a narrow road', and not many people choose it.

It occurs to me that Jesus said that the entrance into his kingdom is narrow. The way to hell, he said, is broad. Why should the entrance to his kingdom be narrow? Could it be that he was saying that you could only get into his kingdom alone? You can't say, 'I will come if my husband comes'. Or, 'I will come if my mates come'. He said, 'If you come at all then you will have to come alone'.

CHAPTER 16

Alone

There is no doubt that you are alone.

When my children were little and were ill, my wife and I would gladly have had the illness ourselves if we could have eased their discomfort by taking it on to ourselves. We suffered deeply because we could only stand by and watch them in pain or distress.

Frank Sinatra sang, 'I did it my way'. Lord George Brown took that song as the theme of his autobiography. If they meant it then I admire them both. Rabbie Burns wished that God would give us grace to see ourselves as others see us.

I worked for nine years as a BBC radio producer. Over and over again when we had recorded someone and then played the recording back for them to hear, they would say, 'Was that really me?'

If you see yourself for the first time on film, your immediate reaction is that you are watching a stranger. How little we know ourselves.

That voice that you hear, or that film that you see, is you. Why do they seem so strange? Could it be that we have a mental image of ourselves that is completely remote from reality? I am imagining that I am being one thing and you are hearing or seeing something entirely different. That is one reason why I don't like the telephone or even writing. I can say something on the phone with a twinkle in my eye but you don't see the twinkle. You can misunderstand me hopelessly.

Take words. I could say, 'I wish you were here,' and that could mean, 'I WISH you were here', or it could mean, 'I wish YOU were here', or, 'I wish you were HERE'.

I almost give up hope that any of us can really communicate what we really mean. We don't actually lie to one another (at least, not all the time), but does anyone ever know the whole truth of what we mean whenever we speak or write?

At a meal with three other people you want the salt. Do you say, 'Please pass me the SALT', or, 'PLEASE pass me the salt', or, 'Please PASS me the salt', or, 'Please pass me the salt (it's by your elbow, you stupid idiot, and can't you see that I want it?)'?

If you ever imagine that you are really communicating with another human being, forget it. The best you can hope for is that they may get a vague idea of what you mean.

If I were to say to a woman, 'I love you', just think of all the permutations that she could read into that. And if I said that to a man and someone overheard what I said, think what they could begin to imagine. How isolated we are when you begin to think about it. I have observed dogs at work relating to other members of the same species, and they don't seem to have any of the complicated problems that we have. Lucky dogs!

There you are then. Probably lonely, certainly alone. Can we capitalize on that? I think that we can.

I must say again that loneliness is bad. It is either due to your failure or due to the failure of the rest of us, your failure because you are afraid of standing alone, or our failure through not recognizing your need.

But aloneness is not destructive. It is very good. It is something that you will have to face eventually, so you might as well get on with it now. You can pretend to yourself that you are not alone by striving never to be lonely, desperately adjusting who you are in order to be liked or accepted. But you know and I know that although you can try to fill every second of every minute of every hour of every day with one distraction or another, there will come that moment when you will realize that you are alone.

It may come at night when your wife or husband is asleep and you are still awake. It may be that because you have no one to sleep with you lie in bed alone. It can come in the day when surrounded by other people you are aware that you are you and that no one else can be who you are.

I am claiming that that experience is not something to run away from. Many people have an overwhelming desire to escape from it. They will cling to anything to avoid it. Let it come. Stand alone. You won't cease to exist.

Of course we need other people to supply our needs for warmth, light and food. In that sense we will always be inter-dependent on each other. Don't be tricked by that into believing that you as a self cannot survive alone.

Watch the world of nature. The baby bird cannot survive without the help of the mother and father bird. The time comes however when the baby bird has to leave the nest.

Someone in the Bible said, 'Look at the ants'. A lonely ant looks terribly alone. Ants seem to survive by submerging their individual identity for the sake of the colony. Isn't that what Fascists say? Isn't that what Communists say? – that you must sacrifice your identity for the good of the whole? I am saying that in such a society you would not be allowed to have any expressible identity that you *could* sacrifice. I dream of a society where each member could say 'I am' because everyone else could say the same about who they were, and we would not need to steal someone else's selfhood in order to survive. Nor would we be dependent upon someone else sacrificing their self for us. Nor would we need to sacrifice who we are in order to gain approval. All the 'games' could stop. I could be me and you could be you and we would both feel secure. What is more I would be enriched by you, and you by me. Any other way must end in one or both being diminished.

That day however has not arrived. We live in a world where total fear of people being who they are is the order of the day. The people who are desperate that I should conform are desperate for the simple reason that they have settled for being a false self in a false world and are afraid of the truth. Afraid of me being me.

'The truth shall make you free,' says the Bible. And so it would. We choose slavery, not freedom. At all costs don't be who you are, says the world. Be what we want you to be, and because you are afraid to stand alone, or because you are afraid that if you do stand alone you will be destroyed, you play the 'game' that the world demands, which destroys you anyway.

Jesus said, 'Except a man be born *again* he will not find the kingdom of heaven'. St Paul said, 'The old man must die in order that the new man can be born'. What did they mean? What is this new self that has to be born? What is this old self that has to die? I have to be born again. Whatever I have been up to that point has to die. Well, what have I been that has to die and what or who is the new me that has to be born?

I start by saying that who I am was created by God. I believe that God is good and anything that he makes must therefore be good. Genesis chapter one verse 31 says, 'God saw everything that he had made and behold it was very good'. But everything on this earth is not very good. Cancer for instance. Brain-damaged children may be good but the brain damage isn't. Lonely, frightened people obviously are not what life was supposed to be. People who want to murder aren't good. Wars aren't good. Lying and stealing and dominating and destroying aren't good. Lots and lots of things that people do are a long way from being good. Something must have gone wrong with creation and particularly with people. I am positive that a great deal of what happens on this planet is not what a good God wanted.

I have no explanation of why there is so much evil on this planet. Everything went wrong somewhere. If you don't believe in a good God who is the creator of the universe, then you have no problem. Whatever happens just happens. There is no rhyme or reason for anything. There is no plan, no purpose, no meaning in the universe. However, if you believe, as I believe, that your whole 'feel' about being alive is that being alive has got a meaning, then you simply must ask where and how did it go wrong?

I don't know why there is cancer, and brain damage and murder and cruelty, except that in every individual case it might one day be explained (we could explain now why it happens in some cases), but why is it there at all? That I don't know. There is evil in the world, that is obvious, but why there is baffles me. All the explanations that I have heard or read by learned people don't convince me, and if I were to list all those explanations here and now, you would get bored before you had heard half of them and so would I. That doesn't alter the fact that this world is in a mess. Why drought? Why famine? Why earthquakes? Why disease? Why the terrible cruelty in the animal world, 'nature red in tooth and claw'? I don't know. The world I see could in places have been created by a good God, for instance, the incredible beauty of a blade of grass. In other places only an evil, malevolent God could have made it, for instance myxomatosis among rabbits.

If you say, as I say, that what God made was very good then something, some time went wrong. Not because God made a mistake originally; it could only be that there is another power at work, an anti-God power who has mucked up the whole thing. That God's original intention will come to pass one day I have no doubt, but in the meantime we have got a problem.

I'm sorry for the apparent diversion. It isn't a diversion actually, because it leads on to me being able to say that I do know one way in which man has gone wrong. That one way could be a clue to why almost everything else has gone wrong.

Jesus said that you must be born again. Whatever you are now has got to die to make way for a new person. What, or who, are you now? You are most likely what the world that you have lived in has made you. If the world is in a mess, then it follows that what the world has made you to be is a mess. And who is so arrogant and conceited that they wouldn't admit that such is the case with them?

The messed-up world has made you who you are. And yet I believe that at the moment of your creation, at that very moment of creation when your father's spermatozoon met your mother's ovum, a person was created who had the potential of being (in God's words) very good.

However, in that spermatozoon and in that ovum lay the potential of not being very good. Nine months in the womb where the messed-up world was affecting you. Birth, where the effect deepened. Growing up when the effect was even more powerful, until now, at this very moment where a messed-up world has made you what you think you are.

I believe that from the start, from the moment of your creation, you did have a choice. You could be what all your inheritance demanded that you should be, i.e. a mess, or be what God had made you, i.e. very good. The odds against the latter are tremendous. Only one person has ever defied those odds and that was Jesus of Nazareth. The fact that he did it gives hope to the rest of us. It can be done through what he did for us. 'Tempted in every way,' says the Bible, 'but he never fell into the fallen ways of a fallen world.'

The Bible says that you must start again. 'You must be born again,' to use its language. 'How can I do this?' you may well ask. A man called Nicodemus asked the same question. 'Do you mean,' he said to Jesus, 'that I must go back into my mother's womb and be born again in that sense?' 'No,' said Jesus, 'it isn't like that.'

Well, what *is* it like?

I'll tell you. Whoever you are now is what 'the world', the messed-up world, has made you. You have been made by 'the world' around you into what that 'world' wants you to be. Jesus said, 'My kingdom is not of *this* world'. How right he was! To be of *this* 'world' is to stagger from one disaster to another.

The only way to survive, most people think, is to be part of 'the world' as it is. So we make our adjustments in order to fit in with what 'the world' demands. Marriage is what 'the world' says it is. Being a child is what 'the world' says a child is. A teenager is what 'the world' expects a teenager to be. To survive as an adult means fitting into what 'the world' demands that you should be. You can't be you, you must be what 'they', i.e. 'the world', say you must be. And all of that is disastrous.

Jesus introduced the greatest revolution of all time. He had the effrontery to say that what 'the world' is, is nothing other than a total disaster. No wonder that 'the world' crucified him! He had the audacity to say that 'the world' as it is will go to hell. He was right then, and he is right now. Let anyone stand by the self that God created, then he or she can't hope for much sympathy from 'the world'. 'The world' can't tolerate it. Did 'the world' of his day accept Jesus with open arms? And St Paul? And Martin Luther? And John Wesley? And Galileo? And many others who had the guts to say, 'Here I stand, I can do no other'? The 'I' was the self that God created which the world hated. Why do you think that the Bible describes the devil as 'the prince of *this* world'? To stand against the devil and 'the world' that is in his power takes enormous guts. Jesus had that.

You know, and I know that you know, that buried somewhere inside you is the self that God made. Until now you may have settled for what 'the world' has asked, no, demanded that you should be. Jesus says that the God-created self that you really are must come to life. All that 'the world' has made you into must die, so that who you really are can come alive.

Jesus said that if this happens, then 'the world' will hate you, in fact it will crucify you as it crucified him.

The odds against our even knowing, never mind living from, the self that God created are enormous. There is no person alive now who can do that on his own. The promise of Jesus, the 'Gospel' – the 'Good News' – is that if that is what you want to be, really want to be, then he is alive to help you. You can make it, not on your own but with him you can. That is the promise.

You won't understand how he did it, nor can I. But somehow when he was hanging on that cross he was making it possible for you to be who God created you to be.

If you allow him into your life, if you allow the 'new' self to come alive (the self that you always could have been from your creation but weren't given the chance to be), then don't expect 'the world' to give you an easy ride. It won't. It will try to destroy you. It may destroy you in terms of fame, glory and success in this world. Who, though, wants to be a messed-up success in this messed-up world? The answer is, most of us. This 'world' is the only world that we know, so what is wrong with being a success within it? Nothing? Except that you will be still-born! You will have no idea of what the 'other' world, 'the kingdom' as Jesus called it, is all about.

When you lie in that coffin, as you surely will, it won't really matter how successful you have been in this 'world', you will have to leave all that behind. Jesus asked us to 'lay up treasures in heaven' which we will not have to leave behind when the soil thuds on our coffin or the gas-jets consume it.

He said that you can start now laying up treasures in heaven. The only way to do that is to become friends with the self that God created, to live in his kingdom here and now. 'Dear God, that is so difficult.' Who said that it wouldn't be? Remember though that you are not fighting for that on your own. The one person who ever did that completely is on your side and he will give you the strength to go on living from that self at times when your own courage fails.

Please then don't let your fear of standing alone stop you from doing it. Make friends with the self that God created and ask Jesus, who was himself, to help you to be just that. 'The world' will attack you, and persecute you and reject you. The wonderful news is that God will do none of those things. 'To thine own self be true,' said Shakespeare. The reward is to have Jesus say to you, 'Enter my kingdom thou good and faithful servant'. Don't kid yourself that achieving that will be easy. It won't. But it can be done.

I'll tell you next how I found out that it is possible.

What I have to say will be very personal and if you can't stand people talking intimately about their deepest experiences, then don't read the next chapter. You will of course, because for you as for me curiosity is a strong and deeply rooted motivation. So, you will read it. But it is your decision to do so, not mine. OK?

Chapter 17

Adventure into Loneliness

By the summer of 1973 I had arrived. I was a fully qualified Methodist minister. I was a fully qualified Anglican priest. For the previous nine years I had had great success as a full-time radio producer for the BBC. I knew a lot of famous people and some of them liked me.

I was married to a very lovely woman whom I loved. I had two delightful children. I had a very nice home and I was earning very good money. I had got it made.

In the autumn of 1973 I resigned from the BBC. They didn't ask me to go, I left. My years with them had been very happy.

For over nine years I knew what it was like to have power. I was important. I was also accepted by people who were more important in the world than I was, and I enjoyed it. I got very close to where real worldly power lies. At least where it appears to lie. Leaders in politics, entertainment, the Church, the trade unions, accepted invitations to work for me. I saw at first hand who they were and what they were like. It created for me a great conflict. Power tends to corrupt and yet someone has to have it. It is all very well for us to castigate some of those in power who have allowed themselves to be compromised. What would you do, I wonder, if you had that power? There is only one person who had ultimate power without being corrupted and that was Jesus. The rest of us, to a greater or lesser extent, fall from virtue.

Politicians are viewed with suspicion and rightly so. 'The price of freedom is eternal vigilance.' But in Britain those I met were good men and women trying to do a good job as honestly as they could. However, in a corrupt world, you will find some corruption everywhere. It must be so. Corruption does not always involve illegality. It can simply mean being false.

In 'Show Biz' there is a lot of worldly power, and the casualty rate in human destruction is high.

In the Church there is power. Sometimes it is worldly power, veneered by a religious cover. Sometimes it is not. It is sad to observe the religious ladder used by people to climb to a higher worldly position. How many of us though wouldn't do that if we were given the chance? 'Let him who is without sin cast the first stone,' said Jesus. There are others in the Church who occupy 'lowly' positions without envy and some who occupy 'high' positions without loss of integrity. The Church (in all denominations) is a very mixed bag.

So, there I was in 1973 in a position of considerable power with countless 'friends'. I put that word 'friend' in inverted commas because there were many who cultivated my 'friendship' because of what I was. I have done the same, so I can't throw any stones, not even a small one.

Then I resigned. I had given what I could to the BBC, and without any kind of pressure from them I left.

Within two weeks of leaving I was in a mental hospital with serious depression. Where the depression came from I do not know. I think I have heard all the theories about what causes depression, but even when you think that you know what has caused yours it doesn't remove the depression. This was where Freud in his early days was so utterly wrong. To relive early experiences under psychoanalysis, or these days under a clinically administered drug, may help you to understand why you are depressed, but that in itself doesn't remove it. It is like saying to a man who has fallen off a ladder and broken his leg, 'I know why your leg is broken, you fell off that ladder'. A fat lot of good that will do.

Six weeks in a mental hospital. Quite an experience. The nursing was first class (and it was on the National Health). The psychiatrists could have helped more, but with so many patients and so few psychiatrists they have to ration their time, consequently no patient can possibly receive the amount of time that he needs. Again, I throw no stone at the psychiatrists. What we need is more of them. We also need much more research into that whole field. We think we know something about what causes mental illness but we know very little about curing it, and there is very little done to stop it happening in the first place.

Take the case of 'George'. Retired, middle 60s, middle class. He arrived in my ward literally shaking with anxiety that became panic. Why? Because the money he had invested wasn't producing enough interest to keep pace with inflation, and he might have to sell his detached house with a garden that he treasured overlooking the sea. He wouldn't be able to go on providing for his wife, whom he loved, what she was accustomed to.

He wasn't mad. He was in a panic. He was given tranquillizers. He talked with me by the hour. He hated being in a mental hospital. The stigma made him feel deeply ashamed. He was intelligent enough to realize that the tranquillizers weren't going to cure his problem or take it away. He was offered Electro-Convulsive Therapy, i.e. electric shocks hammered through the brain when the patient is unconscious. In desperation he accepted the offer. After that treatment he was calmer. A week later he went home. A few weeks after arriving home he jumped off a cliff. Did he kill himself? Or did society, which means you and me, kill him?

Then there was 'Marjorie'. A patient because she had slashed her wrists. She received the treatment, went home and was soon back with slashed legs. Why was she trying to destroy herself?

And 'Betty', whose adored husband had been killed in an accident that wasn't his fault. She received financial compensation. She was a patient because her life was an empty void without meaning or purpose. 'All you need is love,' sang the Beatles. But who was going to give her the love she needed to fill the gap in her heart that the death of her husband had left? Tablets? ECT? That's what she got, plus the psychiatrist telling her that there was nothing really wrong with her. He was right in the sense that she suffered from something that tablets would never cure. Nor ECT. Her heart was broken. How do you mend a broken heart?

And 'Philip'. Young, intelligent, charming and rather quiet. Until the night that he smashed open the drug cupboard in a violent rage and was overpowered just before he had taken enough tablets to kill himself. We never saw him again. The rumour said that he had been taken to Ward 'X', a place we were all frightened of in case *we* ended up there. We didn't know what happened to people in Ward 'X', but whatever it was, the fear of Ward 'X' was passed on by us to each new patient who arrived in our ward, and in turn they would pass it on to new patients who arrived after them.

I used to lie awake asking myself, 'Are you really mad? You must be or you wouldn't be in this place. But I'm not mad. Are you sure? And who is this you anyway?'

By this stage my marriage had ceased to function. Drained dry by my work at the BBC (my fault, not theirs), depressed and drinking more than was good for me, I really wasn't fit to live with.

After six weeks in the mental hospital I headed back to London to look for work. My wife and children at this stage were living in Cornwall. Friends took me in. Christopher and Pam Martin were saints. What they had to put up with is between them and me, but my love and gratitude for them could never die.

My wife and children were marvellous. I went back to Cornwall from time to time to be with them, but in Cornwall there was no work for me. The Church was more than dubious about offering me a job.

Twice more in mental hospital with the same problem. The psychiatrist turned to his last hope, Electro-Convulsive Therapy. That didn't work either. In between times I drifted around looking for a job. I am what is called a 'Laughing Depressive'. That means that when you feel that life is absolutely 'bloody' you can still laugh at the absurdity of it all.

When the nurse in the mental hospital woke me up to give me sleeping tablets I wasn't angry, but I nearly died laughing. Bless her, she was carrying out her orders. Mr Trevivian must have his tablets, the rules say so.

I went to one Labour Exchange where the man wrote down very carefully all my qualifications. Then he went away and came back with information about a job vacancy. If I remember rightly, it was to make the tea for the typists in the Income Tax Office. I hurried round there and after being interviewed was turned down. I actually smiled as I walked away. A few months before a future Prime Minister had been my guest, now I wasn't even good enough to brew a pot of tea.

So the months dragged on. Labour Exchanges, drawing the dole, applying for jobs, mental hospital, visits to psychiatrists, and the number of 'friends' dwindling rapidly.

I won't dwell on what happened in Africa where I went for one job and was put into *their* mental hospital. A locked ward with 30 Africans some of whom were violent and hated me because I was a white xxxxxxx!

Well, what would you do? No job, no home, no money; only a tiny number of friends including my wife and children, my sister and her husband and my parents – but I couldn't live with them although they cared. Even those I tended to keep away from. There comes a time when you just can't go on accepting other people's time and patience and in some cases money.

Well, what do you then *do*?

Even worse, you begin to ask, 'Who am I?' I had always been a somebody. I had been a clergyman. I had been a husband. I had been a father. I had been a BBC producer. In the past I had a home. I had never been without a few bob. All I had now was Social Security.

'Who am I?' I asked. I was still alive, but as what? 'Who is Roy Trevivian?' I asked.

Throughout all this my faith in the living presence of Jesus Christ didn't waver. He didn't seem to be doing anything but I never doubted that he was there.

I ended up in a place called Pilsdon in Dorset. A large house with seven and a half acres of land which a friend of mine, Percy Smith, had taken over 18 years before. His aim was to provide a place where broken and lost human beings could go and live. The accommodation wasn't wonderful. Mine was a converted horse-box next to where sick pigs were kept! Not all Percy's pigs were sick, the vast majority were completely fit, it was just two or three sick ones who lived next to me. They kept on grunting all through the night.

Through the day there was work. Manual work. I chopped logs. Well, not actually chopped them, they were too big for that. I had to drive steel wedges into them with a sledge-hammer in order to split them. Back-breaking work. No pay, you worked for your keep. I have no complaints. Prayers four times a day, quite voluntary, but I never missed them. Why pray to a Jesus who hadn't cured my depression, who hadn't found me a job, who hadn't reunited me with my family, who had appeared in fact to do precisely nothing? Why? Because he knew what it was all about and what he was doing. It was only later on that I realized how true that was. I was at Pilsdon for six months. The depression never eased but my body became healthier.

What I did find though was the greatest treasure of all. I was still alive. Not as anybody, simply alive. I ached to be with my family, but to be with them wouldn't have helped them. My son came to stay with me for two weeks and that was marvellous. But I wasn't fit to belong to a family and live within a family situation. When my son came to visit me he was only 13, but he came without judgement or condemnation. Apart from my son, who stayed for two weeks on two occasions, I had four other one-day visitors in six months. I am not complaining. For most of the time, although I was part of a community of 30 people, I was alone.

At first I felt lonely. I felt depressed. I experienced my fair share of self-pity. I shed many tears. I went to bed with my body actually feeling the physical pain of loneliness. Often the pain made sleep impossible, but when I did sleep the pain returned when I awoke.

I lived with the pain (the physical pain) of loneliness as my permanent companion. I still have it from time to time.

Gradually through the pain of loneliness a light began to dawn. The faintest, smallest flicker of a dawn. In 'the world' I was a nobody. A horse-box for my home; a sledge-hammer for my work (I was 54!). Who were all the 'important' people whom I had known? Who was the me that they had known? That me had gone. There were now no props to bolster up a me that needed props. There was only me, and Jesus. Yes, there was Jesus. He was there in the Pilsdon chapel four times a day and eventually throughout the days, and he was there through the long sleepless nights, with the pigs grunting their heads off.

No, he didn't take the pain away. He never has completely. It is with me now as I am writing this book. In spite of the pain though, I know that I am me and he is Jesus. If losing the pain means losing him, then I'll keep the pain.

After five months at Pilsdon I decided that 'I' was strong enough to face the world again. I applied through the post for 47 jobs. This job I now have was the very first I applied for (through the kind help of Peter, whose work it is to find jobs for clergymen who don't really fit the clergy scene). I was finally offered four jobs. The other three paid more than this one. I chose the job I am now doing. Or rather, I didn't choose this job. I prayed about which one I should choose. I put up a hard fight for the one that paid the most. I don't expect you to believe me when I tell you what I chose, why should you? ('All men are liars,' says Psalm 116.) I wanted to provide the most I could for my wife and my children. In the event Jesus said that it was to here that I must go. How did I know that? Because if you truly believe that he is there and you truly ask him to tell you, then he will. He told me.

So here I am and I have been here for two and a half years. My wife and daughter still live in Cornwall. My son lives with me here, and the East End folk among whom I live accept me for who I am.

Yes, I do at times feel lonely. Terribly lonely. Yet somehow I know that out of loneliness, if you can face it, and if you can renounce self-pity, and if you can overcome the great urge to blame other people, then there can come a strange but wonderful experience of being alone.

You don't love other people less. In true aloneness you love them more. You stand alone and out of the freedom that you now have you can give without needing a return. You never strike a bargain like 'If you love me then I will love you'. You simply say, 'I love you whether you love me or not'. Of course you can't do it all the time. Only Jesus could and can do that. Of course it hurts when having loved you get smashed in the teeth as your reward, and you are tempted to say, 'Never again'. By and large, though, because you have learned to be alone, your need to be loved by other human beings lessens. I still need Jesus though and always will. He went all the way alone, and because he could go all the way, he can love you as no other person will ever be able to.

I still need him. I don't know why this should be. It is the way that God the Creator made us. To go into aloneness without Jesus could drive a person mad and even to suicide.

Don't seek aloneness unless you enter that with him. He could take it, you can't. I have known people who have gone into loneliness and on into aloneness without him, and as far as this life is concerned, 'they' have ceased to exist, even though their bodies have stayed alive.

However, with him, it is in aloneness that the real treasures lie. You will find him in a way that otherwise you would not. You will love in a way that otherwise you could not. You will find what it is to be a real human being. I have only started the journey but I know the path, and I know that following it is what being alive is all about.

CHAPTER 18

The Diminishment Game

Shakespeare said, 'a rose by any other name would smell as sweet'. And so it would. It would look the same and smell the same even if you called it 'a dungwort'.

Does that mean that names don't matter at all? I think they do matter.

For many years I have been irritated by the use of nicknames. Of course nicknames can simply be terms of affection and endearment. When my daughter was born many ladies in the church who wanted to give her a present knitted for her pairs of woollen bootees. Somehow she became known to us as 'Booty', then 'Bootsie', then 'Boo' and then for some unfathomable reason she became 'Blue'. Her name is Carolyn and that became Caro! All quite harmless, you are saying. Why are you going to make a fuss? I am. I don't like it.

When I address you, it is you to whom I am speaking and if I call you 'Lofty' or 'Pip' or 'Chalky' or 'Titch' or some variant of your first name or surname, then in the subtlest way I am, without realizing it, denying you your true identity.

At baptism a child is given a Christian name. The child is no longer just the son or daughter of their parents, the child is now acknowledged as belonging to God, and it is only God to whom we can ever rightly say that we do belong.

There was a time when the Christian name of a child was never divulged by the parents until the moment of baptism. It was believed that if a witch, or the devil, could discover the name of the child before baptism, then the name could be used to put an evil spell on the child. To know the name was to have power over the child. There is an echo of this in the Church of England's Baptismal

Service. Just before the water is poured over the child's head and the child is baptized, the priest says, 'Name this child,' and it was at that point and only at that point in the past that the name was divulged. Now we can say that all that was just silly superstition. Well it might be, but behind every superstition there is a speck of rational significance. In this case the business of not declaring the name of the child before the moment of baptism was simply saying that the name of the child has some significance.

Recently I watched a serial on TV called 'Roots'. It was a true story about a teenaged African boy who was captured by slavers, taken to America and there sold to a farmer. The boy's real name was Kunta Kinte. It was the practice of people who bought a slave to give the slave a new name. They called Kunta by the name Toby. He refused to accept the new name and showed his hatred of being a slave. He clung to his real name. So the owner had him tied to a whipping post. The flogging was hideous. Eventually, at the point of collapse when the agony of the whip had almost destroyed him, he whispered, 'My name is Toby'. They almost flogged his identity out of him. From then on, his selfhood almost gone, he became what his owner wanted, an apparently servile, broken, obedient slave. After his death Kunta's daughter, who hadn't seen him for a long time, found his grave. The grave was marked with a stone which had inscribed upon it the name Toby. She knelt by the grave and sobbed. Then she picked up a piece of chalky rock and struck out the name Toby and with the rocky chalk she scrawled the name Kunta Kinte. I found the whole episode deeply moving. She gave him back his full identity.

In the war privates were called collectively 'bods', short for bodies. Some generals would find it easier to order 10,000 'bods' or 'troops' into battle where several thousands of them would be slaughtered. What general could have sent Fred and Jack and Tom and Harold and Arthur, men whose names he knew, out to be slaughtered? I don't blame the generals. Some of them hated the death of even one of their men. Could the war have been fought with men who had names? I doubt it. To know my name is to have some sort of relationship with me, making it more difficult for you to kill me. It is much easier to kill 'the enemy' instead of Karl or Günther or Hans. But war destroys people, that is the object, so names had to go.

And what is all this fuss about nicknames, you are thinking? Well, a nickname can be a way of diminishing you, or if it is 'Lofty' or 'Titch' or 'Sandy' then the nickname is only describing a part of you. When you call me Roy I feel that you are speaking to me, all of who I am. Because I am a clergyman I sometimes get called 'Reverend', but that isn't me, it is one of my functions.

In the Bible, in St John's gospel, chapter 10 verse 4, Jesus says that because he is the Good Shepherd 'He calls his own sheep by name'. I suppose that the first person to whom Jesus gave a name was a man called Simon, and when Jesus looked right into that man's heart and saw who he really was, Jesus said, 'You are not Simon, you are Peter,' and Peter meant 'rock', and although Peter at that time was utterly unstable the time came when Peter did become the person that God had created, and a rock Peter became.

When the angel told Mary that she was going to have a baby the angel said that the baby was to be named Jesus. And Jesus he was and still is, and that name meant saviour.

When Jesus cured the madman who was possessed by evil spirits, he asked the man, 'What is your name?' But the man hadn't got a name because his identity had almost been destroyed, but from the mouth of the man came the voice of the evil spirit which possessed him saying, 'My name is Legion,' and Jesus cast out Legion and the man became himself, and as the Bible says, the man returned to his right mind. It was in knowing the name of the evil spirit that Jesus had power over it.

I shudder when I hear men refer to 'the wife' or 'the missus'. No woman is simply a wife and no man is only a husband. Each wife or husband is a person, with an individual, separate identity; with a name. We often get it right on tombstones or gravestones: 'Here lies Hannah, the wife of Albert Jackson'. No one would think of simply inscribing, 'Here lies the wife of Albert Jackson'. We know instinctively that such an inscription would be wrong. We get it right in death, why not in life? Could it be that at the time of death there is nothing left that belongs only to this world? – there is only what God created, a person, someone with his own individual identity.

Not calling someone by his individual name is often done unthinkingly. Often, though, it is when we act without thinking that we give away our true attitudes. If, then, I feel insecure about my identity as an individual human being, unable to stand alone, then probably I would prefer you to call me by something other than my true name and I would prefer to avoid yours.

I have written at some length about the way we diminish each other in the way we address one another. That is because I have rather a 'thing' about nicknames. There are however other ways in which we diminish one another, ways in which we fail to give each other our true value as human beings and thereby add to the general loneliness that people feel.

When a controversial matter is being discussed, if I have more aggression than you, or have a stronger personality, then I can dominate the discussion and make you feel very small. Or because you only see me through your own eyes and your experience, you may fail completely to see my point of view, and I am left feeling completely misunderstood and horribly isolated.

The blaming game can be very destructive. Has there ever been a wrong committed that was totally the responsibility of one person? I doubt it. There are always many other factors and many other people who have made their contribution. Of course there is always a prime mover, but the other factors and other people are almost always forgotten. A teenaged boy from my neighbourhood breaks into a shop and steals. Of course he is to blame. But only him? Had his father ever stolen anything? Does he live in an environment where stealing is accepted? Was his education such as to fit him for a decent job? Are there any jobs around anyway, decent or not? I am not pleading to exonerate the lawbreaker, but I often feel that as the prime mover he is carrying the blame for many other people and a whole host of circumstances. Of course deep within him he knows this, and feels he is being treated unjustly, and that feeling shuts him off from society. Jesus knew all about this kind of isolation and diminishment when he took upon himself the sins and desolation of the whole world, in spite of his total innocence.

I was in a group of people the other day when one man said that it was normal to be married. Little did he know that in that group was a woman of mature years who was not married. Later she told me how deeply he had hurt her, implying that she was not normal, and also implying that in some way she was less than a human being. He didn't intend to hurt her, but that was precisely what he had done. He had as good as said that she didn't belong to normal society, and if she was already feeling that then what he said could only have made her feel even more isolated.

I have a friend who believes that he is sexually unattractive. I have no way of judging whether he is or not. Women tell me that he is wrong, but he will not believe this. It doesn't help when his wife is with him and she constantly remarks about how handsome other men are. She may not realize that she is diminishing his self-confidence all the time, but she is.

There are some women who are married to clergymen and who revel in that fact. But I know others who resent deeply being treated as a 'clergy wife'. They protest that they can never be themselves, but have to live up to whatever people's image is of what the wife of a clergyman should be. I remember the wife of a policeman who lived near me, and she once spilled out to me her burning resentment because the other women kept her at a distance. I find authority figures difficult to cope with, and once when I met the wife of a bishop I scorned her with the words, 'Hm! a bishop's wife'. And I saw the tears come into her eyes as she murmured, 'My name is Joan'. I felt dreadful. But we all do it, a lot of the time. We put people into classes, categories, groups, roles and fail to value the individual to whom we are doing this.

The only way I know of defeating the diminishment game, is to remind myself whenever I treat someone as less than a human being in their own right, that Jesus loves that person just as much as he loves me and probably more.

CHAPTER 19

Alone and Together

You may be thinking that I am claiming that the final and complete state of being human is to be able to stand alone. I am not claiming that. What I am claiming is that until you have arrived there you will never know what a true relationship with someone else can be.

All relationships that start with need and go on with need are doomed. It is so obvious. 'You have to be what I want you to be.' Or 'I must be what you want'. How can either of us be ourselves? To go that way is to live with totally phoney relationships which become sour and horrible. You can see them all around you – people sucking each other's blood.

The advertisers want me to want their product. Are they doing that because they love me? Nonsense. True advertisers (and there are some) are offering me a choice and that is good. However, to manipulate me with advertising techniques is not to give me a choice, it is aimed at giving me no choice except what they choose I must want.

We do this with each other. We will go to any lengths to catch and hold someone we want. A man I know whose wife has left him told me that he would crawl on his hands and knees to where she lives, if only she would have him back. Another man I know whose wife has left him has told me that there is nothing he wouldn't do to get her back. Why is it always men who say these things and rarely women? For all their demands for liberation, women seem to be far more independent and more able to stand alone than men. In the last war, when I went to a dance it was always the man who had to risk rejection by asking the girl if she would dance with him. Only this week, a young man was complaining to me that it was always him who had to ask a girl for a date, never the other way round. And he hasn't got two heads. In fact he's quite handsome.

However, what we do is to fasten on to other human beings, or one other human being, and use them to help us to survive. It never really works. There is always the gnawing anxiety that they may go away. Shakespeare's Julius Caesar said it in the words, *Et tu Brute* meaning, 'Even you, Brutus, my dearest friend, are helping my enemies to stab me to death'. Remember too that whoever it is upon whom you are dependent will have to leave you when they die, as they will. Or you will have to leave them when your eyes close for the last time.

Inter-dependency will always be necessary. There are some people without whom none of us could go on living at all – for instance, people who make the provision of food possible.

Dependency however, and that is what I am writing about, says that I, as a person, as a self, could not exist without you. But I can. It takes a long time to reach that state. In the womb you couldn't stay alive without your mother. After birth there are dependencies that are necessary. You need loving and treasuring in order to grow as a person. Someone has to teach you to read and write. The final aim, though, must be to reach the stage where as a person you can throw off all dependencies because you are able to say 'I am' and not be afraid of being alone.

This does not mean that because you have accepted your separateness you now stand aloof from everybody else. What it does mean is that you can make relationships without needing to manipulate the other person to make your own survival possible. We all have a great need to relate. We grow in relationships, we learn through relating. The big question is, what kind of relationships are we looking for? Not those that tie people together and in doing so make each party become diminished. We should relate out of freedom, the freedom that comes from being able to stand alone if necessary, without fear or anxiety.

Relationships of that quality create nothing but what is good. Few people actually get all the way there, but without doubt that is the goal. Anything less must eventually produce resentment and hate. Do you really respect anyone who would be your slave in order to hold on to you? Do you as a slave really love the one to whom you are bound in slavery? You will be suspicious of them, you will hate them because they cannot be all the time what you want them to be.

'Worldly' love has a lot of hate in it; a lot of jealousy; a lot of possessiveness. All of them are destructive. Christian love, or Christ-like love, is saying that out of my freedom I am choosing to love you and choosing to let you love me. There are no ties in Christian love, no compulsions, only free choice.

'Falling in love' is exciting and wonderfully romantic and all-absorbing, but finally it is a sickness. We describe people who are 'in love' as 'love-sick', and we are using the right word. It isn't very harmful, but it has got some dangers. To use the word 'fall' is to imply an accident, something over which you have no control. To be able from time to time to experience total abandonment, to feel 'taken over' or, to use modern pop language 'to be sent', is all right in small doses. But look at the dangers implied. You are being taken over, you are being carried along by a power beyond your control, you have become a slave.

It is common for middle-aged married people to fall in love with someone other than their partner. Often it is with someone younger. An attempt to re-capture a lost youth? These infatuations, for that is what they are, almost always end in disaster. Marriages get smashed, children are deserted and when the infatuation wears off and you see yourself for the idiot you have been, it may be too late to repair the damage.

Older men can sometimes sweep a young girl off her feet. Who are the men really loving when they do this? The girl or themselves? When a young girl falls in love with an older man, of course he shouldn't be brutal and just push her away. What he must do is to accept the infatuation but not use it to lead her to a disaster. It isn't easy because middle-aged men often have the need to prove that they are still men, and what could be more flattering than to have a beautiful young girl in love with them? The question that the older man has to ask is, 'Who am I loving?' A Christian has no choice. He must not be loving himself. His love for the girl and what is in her best interests should govern his responses.

The man who has not really grown up, who is still looking for affirmation of his value from 'the world', will get into a hopeless tangle. The man who knows that his true value lies in the fact that Jesus loves him can ride the storms, and then no one and no relationship will become destructive. Turn all that round and think about women. They do the same. The woman of 40 or 50 enjoys the sensation of a younger man falling for her. Is it the mother he never had that he falls for? Is it her need to persuade herself that the relentless years are not passing?

I was talking to a friend of mine (the Warden here, the Rev. Roger Sainsbury), describing the miseries of loneliness and the bliss of solitude, and he said, 'I love to be with other people but I also love to be alone'. One doesn't have to exclude the other. In fact to be able to be alone enriches all other relationships.

Our present idea of marriage is a nonsense. The Church of England Prayer Book asks the man and the woman 'to forsake all others' except each other. Here are the actual questions that the bridegrooms must answer in thousands of churches every Saturday all over the world:

> 'Joe Bloggs, wilt thou have this woman to thy wedded wife, to live together after God's ordinance in the holy estate of matrimony? Wilt thou love her, comfort her, honour and keep her in sickness and in health AND FORSAKING ALL OTHER, KEEP THEE ONLY UNTO HER (the capitals are mine) so long as ye both shall live?'

And Joe Bloggs has to say, 'I will'.

The bride is asked the same long question, except that for her the question, if they use the old service, includes 'Will you obey Joe Bloggs?' as well as everything else, and she has to say, 'I will'.

The implication of those questions could appear to

imply that one human being can totally satisfy all that another human being requires in every conceivable kind of situation.

What absolute nonsense. Yet there are tens of thousands of marriages, if not millions, where one partner or the other demands that what they imagine the Prayer Book promises mean are kept.

'Forsaking all other'? My wife is an artist, I am not. She needs the companionship of other artists and some of them may be men. I love cricket. I play it and go to watch it and I never do either on my own. Has my wife got to drag herself along with me whenever I am involved in cricket, and be bored out of her mind? Just to ask that is enough to make those words of the marriage ceremony seem to be ridiculous. What the Prayer Book means is that you will not lust sexually for someone else.

I have got several women friends. Is being with them a sin and a breaking of my marriage vows? My wife has men friends whose company she enjoys. Is being with them a sin that she is committing? My answer to both questions is no.

What the Prayer Book means is that you should not have sexual intercourse with anyone other than the one you are married to, and I agree. The Prayer Book means that marriage involves working out the heights and depths of a human relationship, and that there just isn't the time or the opportunity to work that out with anyone else, and of course it is right. It does not mean that you must forsake everyone else, living within what will become a claustrophobic relationship with one other person of the opposite sex. Marriages like that lead to frustration and increasingly to break-up, so that the very idea of the family unit as the right environment in which children should grow up and be developed is being undermined.

Often I have observed some husbands reacting to their wives by saying in effect, 'You are mine, Mine, MINE', as though their wives were a possession (and some wives do the same with their husbands). What we should be saying is, 'Let us enjoy what we have in common, but there will be other people who satisfy that interest of yours that I cannot satisfy'. No one human being can 'meet' another human being at all levels and in all interests.

Because we have bodies, there should be one physical activity that husband and wife share together that is not shared with anyone else. Jesus said that the one thing that husband and wife should share with no one but each other is sexual intercourse. Jesus said that there was only one reason for divorce and that was adultery; which means having sexual intercourse either actually or in fantasy with anyone else other than the person to whom you are married.

I believe that what he was saying was that sexual intercourse is a sacrament, and a sacrament is the outward and visible sign of a spiritual fact. Sexual intercourse between one man and one woman is saying that it is with you and only with you that I can share the depths and riches of what a man and a woman can experience together as two free human beings. The practical fact, as I have already said, is that there is neither the time nor the opportunity to work that out with anyone else.

People, then, who 'sleep around' are simply playing about with what a true relationship between one man and one woman is all about. If you have 'slept around' before you got married, what is there left that can uniquely be the outward and physical expression of your commitment to each other?

If you are married and you are having sexual intercourse with anyone but your wife or husband, then you are throwing away the one thing that expresses your total commitment to each other. You may feel that it is enriching to have sex with someone else. I am saying that it is not. I am saying that to want to share physical sex with someone other than the one you are married to means that your marriage is in danger, or that having sex with someone else will make it increasingly so.

What, however, can be said to someone who has had pre-marital sexual intercourse or has been unfaithful to their marriage partner? Is all lost? Of course not. Something very precious has been lost and no amount of remorse or repentance or forgiveness can alter that, but there is a place for forgiveness and understanding. It isn't true that 'to understand all is to forgive all'. There can be no forgiveness without repentance. You cannot forgive someone who believes that what they have done is not wrong.

To make up for the loss of that unique expression of love, that should only rightly belong to two people who are married, requires a great depth of love and understanding on both sides. If the people concerned think that sexual intercourse is of no real consequence and that relationships aren't affected by it either within or outside marriage, then what I am saying will appear old-fashioned, out-of-date nonsense.

However, I have seen too much hurt caused to too many people when that attitude has been taken.

Of course you can make a good, happy marriage, even if you have had pre-marital sex, but either you will have to keep that a secret or find a partner whose love for you is bigger than the hurt it will cause them when you tell them.

Of course it isn't the end of your marriage if you have committed adultery, but it could be. Your partner will need to love you very deeply to overcome the hurt. A great deal of deep understanding is needed to heal that hurt, and not just by the apparently offended one. There is rarely one totally innocent party and one totally guilty. The apparently innocent party could have contributed by mindless neglect to what the other has done. In the kingdom of Jesus every broken or damaged relationship is redeemable if his love is taken as the yardstick for ours.

But don't throw sexual intercourse away, either before marriage or after marriage. Don't underestimate the damage that doing that can cause. Don't be led by the nose by this permissive age. People pretend that sexual intercourse doesn't matter, in order to appear to be 'with it'. I know the secrets of too many so-called 'with it' people to fall for that one.

So I am saying two things. Sexual intercourse is precious so treasure it. If you have been party to using it wrongly, do not despair. 'Neither do I condemn you,' said Jesus, 'but don't do it again.'

I have officiated at scores of marriages when I knew that the marriage wouldn't work, because the motivation for it was possessiveness. There are thousands of marriages like that which will never work out. Be careful, though, if because I am saying this you are encouraged to think that yours was a mistake. That could be a lovely 'cop-out' from the trauma of finding out who you are and who your partner is. Because you cannot face the pain of being alone and allow your partner to find his or her aloneness, you may run away and ditch him or her. Then you will probably start again with someone else and eventually arrive back at full circle with the situation that you ran away from originally.

The great secret is to be able to get into the other person's mind, instead of being locked inside your own ego. Because you have found out who you are, you can afford to find out who someone else is. You then won't feel threatened by who they are.

All the vicious arguments and conflicts that go on between people would cease to be destructive once we could get out of our own ego and see the world as the other person sees it. However, you can't do that, unless you feel so secure in the knowledge that Jesus loves you that you can afford to come out from behind your own defences and your ploys that attempt to force other people to love you or agree with you. Only the people who are sure that they are loved by Jesus can afford to allow other people to be who they are.

To be able to be alone never means that you will be cut off from other people. Loneliness does that. Aloneness means that you can relate to every other human being without the fear that they may devour you or that you may devour them.

Aloneness, then, is not a road to selfishness. On the contrary it is a door that opens into a world of many valuable and enriching relationships. Enriching for you and enriching for them.

How I long for people who want to know me without my feeling that they are doing it because without my friendship they would feel bereft, lonely and abandoned. I try to turn to other people, not to gobble them up, but because being with them will enrich us both. At least I can say that being with them will enrich me. If they don't want me, so be it. That doesn't destroy me. I know that I am loved by Jesus, so I can offer myself to anyone, and if they accept me then that is fine, and if they don't, then I will not disintegrate.

I keep saying that the clue to this whole business of being who I am and relating to who you are is Jesus. That is a fact. Many people have trodden the path that I have indicated without him. They have found that it has not worked out. That is not a statement, it is a description of what I have observed. It is experiential, not theoretical.

If it is the case that Jesus came into the world, did what he did, and is alive now, in order that we should become what God, the creator of the whole universe, intended us to become, then it seems obvious to me that I cannot become me and you cannot become you without him.

If you think or believe that there is no creator God, then nothing that I am saying can be of any help to you at all.

On the other hand, if you believe, even in the slightest sense, that the creator-God idea could be in the least way remotely true, then mark well what I am saying.

A little while ago I was sitting in a club with a friend. There was a cabaret. One 'act' was a man and woman, with him being 'funny' and her being 'straight'. He was very funny. He did the lot: the stand-up comic routine with jokes, impressions, comic dialogue with his partner, comic dancing routines. He made me laugh. Later I saw them sitting at a table nearby on their own. I think they were married but neither spoke. The face of the man who had made me laugh so much now looked strained and drawn. A face filled with the misery of loneliness and despair. And yet he earned a living making other people laugh! She looked 'empty'. Her eyes were wandering about – they met mine – we held each other's eyes and she asked the question. I am not being funny, but women don't ask me that question these days. I couldn't help feeling how desperate her need must be if she had to turn to me, someone she didn't even know, someone who certainly isn't God's gift to women in that sense. But her eyes were looking, looking for someone, anyone who would show an interest. Yet there was her man only six inches away, he in the despair of his own pool of loneliness and she in hers.

How do you begin to say to such people, 'If only you could understand that Jesus loves you, then you could start again with each other and learn what loving someone else is really all about'? There was no way I could say that without taking the most appalling risks of being misunderstood in many different ways. Jesus took those risks and even he was misunderstood.

Oh! God, what can I say to someone reading this now who is sinking deeper and deeper into the well of loneliness? . . .

You are lonely. That should not be.

You are afraid to be alone. I don't blame you.

Please, though, stop listening to 'the world' with all its facile beckonings. 'Don't feel lonely,' they say, and they invite you to a party where the pain of loneliness strikes even deeper. 'Don't be alone,' they say, 'because you won't need us then, and you must need us or we will be lost because we can't bear not to be needed', and you let them drag you into their emptiness.

Of course, 'they' want you to remain one of 'them'. If you opt out you arouse in 'them' the guilt that they feel for not being able to abandon loneliness themselves. 'They' are afraid that you may find the peace of aloneness that may threaten the phoney 'belonging' that they hang on to. This is certainly true of men who drink in groups. It is usually the same group, and they all drink too much and are secretly guilty about it. If one of the group tries to cut down on his drinking or cut it out altogether, the others feel threatened. Their guilt is stirred up. They often then try to get him back. 'Hello, Jack, care for a drink?' 'No, I've packed it up.' 'Oh! come on, one drink won't do you any harm, have a half.' And unless he is very strong-willed he accepts the invitation and goes back on the old miserable treadmill that he tried to abandon. If that doesn't happen, then he will find that his old drinking pals are no longer his pals. They never really did have anything in common, except the booze and their guilt for depending on it. I know the truth of all that from bitter experience!

Who else could 'they' be apart from those who insist that you belong to them? It could simply be one other human being. It could be your class, your cultural equals, your family, relatives or society generally. It may be those whose skin is the same colour as yours.

They can all be 'they' and they all demand that you stay within the circle that they have drawn for you. Only it isn't a circle, it is a solitary confinement cell.

Do you do this to other people? Are you 'they' for someone else?

None of this is what I observe as I watch the behaviour of Jesus as recorded by reputable historians. He was the friend of the outcast and the successful, of the popular and the 'lonely', of the working man and the capitalist, of the married and the unmarried, of the moral and the immoral, of the terrorist and the law men, of the crook and the judge, of the children and the grown-ups, of the sick and the healthy, of the sane and the mad, of the one who denied him and the one who betrayed him, but none of them, not one of them, could use him for their own ends.

He didn't want to know what you are, but who you are. What you are has been made by this 'world'. Who you are was created by God.

So, when I look to you and ask to be your friend, it isn't what you are that should draw me but who you are. To relate to another human being and be able to say all the time 'I am', and hear you say in words or attitude, 'I also am me' and for both of us to be able to accept that of each other, then for me that is like being able to taste what heaven is all about.

I haven't arrived in heaven in this way, but I have touched it. Only one person lived all the time in that heaven on this earth and he was called Jesus. As it was then so it is now, I cannot make him be what I want him to be. I have to relate to who he is. And he accepts me for who I am.

Close he will always be, but also separate, distinct, himself. His spirit can come alive within me, a spirit that speaks of love and hope and freedom and courage, but it will be his spirit.

When he rose from the dead, the first person to recognize him was a woman, Mary Magdalene. She wanted to hug him. He said 'No'. He said something about not yet having ascended. He didn't push her away but she was trying, as we all do try, to bind him to this 'world'. He said, 'No, I am free and you must learn to be free'.

Any relationship based on what this 'world' demands, that ties and locks us in a cell, is doomed. But it is so difficult to avoid doing that. We all have patches of terrible loneliness. Patches of feeling so meaningless in this vast universe. We feel horribly insecure. Sometimes we will go to any lengths to hold on to each other, even though it is destroying us both.

This is why Jesus is so vitally important. You can call him to your aid and he will come, but you can't own him. He will be there whenever you need him, but you cannot put him in a box (the origin of 'Jack-in-the-box') or keep him in a charm bracelet and carry him around with you. To relate to him is not like having a rabbit's foot for good luck!

I know of a widow whose husband had been in great demand as a preacher: meetings all over the country every day of the week, he was rarely at home. When he was dead and in his coffin she was heard to murmur, 'Now you are mine'. What deep and terrible irony. Now that you are dead you are mine! But we all know how she felt. She spoke for all of us who need to love and be loved. We cannot afford the person we love to be something other than we need. We have to destroy them in order to possess them.

There must be another way.

There is. It begins when you accept that you belong to

and are loved by Jesus. That being alone in this 'world' will not destroy you. To know this is to be free. To know this is to revel in the freedom of those you love.

Who are you? Who am I? We are loved by Jesus Christ and in his love we can truly love each other. Hallelujah!

This is what after twenty-four years of being married my wife and I are beginning to find. For years the marriage was fine. Lots of happiness, lots of fun, then two children who added great richness to what was already a good marriage. Then the marriage began to pall. I became more and more possessive, and as a consequence more and more jealous. Along with this, dependency deepened and with that a growing anxiety that I would lose her. Without realizing what I was doing I created a claustrophobic atmosphere in which she had to live. This could not go on. She had, rightly, had enough. We parted. The relationship didn't break, it never has, but she needed space and air, and only by my leaving could she have it. Apart from having married in the first place, this was the best thing that we ever did. It would have been no good telling me that three years ago. I hated the separation. There were times that I felt I couldn't take it any more. But I had a choice. To go back and make her life a misery, to commit suicide, or to explore the depths of loneliness. I finally chose the latter.

And the result? There is a quality and depth of love between us now that we would never have known had we just clung to each other. That would not only have diminished us both, it would have destroyed our marriage and our relationship. But, my God, it has been tough going. Time and again we have been tempted to return to the old pattern of dependency, but thank God we loved each other enough to see that claustrophobic dependency for the terrible evil that it was. So it is now out of freedom that we love each other. It is through standing within our individual aloneness that we can afford to be together.

I am not of course suggesting that all marriages have the problems of dependency that we had. I am not suggesting that all married couples have to part in order to find in their aloneness what their true selves are. But I can say to those who know that they are destroying each other, that there is another way, other than allowing the destruction with all the allied phenomena of hate, and panic and physical or verbal violence, plus emotional blackmail, to continue. But knowing now the signs of the destructiveness that can exist within marriage, I can report from my observation of many, many marriages that those signs are present in a lot of cases.

To give each other freedom and space, to break free from dependency is a hard and a very tough road, and the temptations to revert are enormous. But either you walk that road with all its pain, and find the freedom and joy that independent love creates, or you continue to wallow in the miseries and hates of clawing each other emotionally to death.

For us, we had to find our central point of reference in Jesus Christ, each in our own way. It was in him that we were able to grow as free individuals and out of that freedom learn to love; to take the risks that are always involved in any journey into freedom. Jesus did say that if we put anyone, and that includes wife, husband, father, mother, child or friend, before him, then all our other relationships are doomed. But if he is first then all our other relationships become gloriously alive. It is strange, that many of us know what he said, but it comes as a great shock when we realize that it is to us that he is speaking, not just to the man or woman next door.

Jesus was obviously against divorce. The social mores of his day weren't the same as ours. In his day a man could easily divorce his wife on the most trivial of grounds. What he said had a lot to do with the protection of women from the capriciousness of men. Even so I believe that any divorce is the admittance of a deep failure. I hold the crazy view that any man could live with any woman in marriage provided the will is there on both sides. But that little word 'will' is the vital one, and 'on both sides' is equally vital. Easier and easier divorce is sapping the will of so many people to actually work at their marriage and thereby discover the wonderful possibilities that it contains. I remember with a smile, and also with a deep sadness, the new wife who came to see me four weeks after I had performed her marriage ceremony. She told me that she was going back to mother. During their courtship her fiancé had never objected to her smoking. After they were married he did. The crunch came when he took a packet of ten cigarettes from her handbag and put them under the cold water tap. Because of that she was going back to mother.

Marriage can be the beginning of a great adventure in relationship. If each is willing to learn, each willing to stand alone, each willing to try to understand the other, great happiness lies ahead. But more and more people are smashing the marriage and the relationship at the first sign of disharmony. It is however through the disharmonies that the relationship can grow and become enriched if they are worked at and through. It is madness for people to grow part-way in a relationship and then because of some problem, great or small, to jettison that relationship without realizing why the breakdown occurred and that the reason for it is not just on one side. If people turn away from the first obstacle that marriage brings, or an obstacle that seems insurmountable, and then marry someone else, the extreme likelihood is that their next marriage will arrive at exactly the same point where the first one broke down.

So I am opposed to easier divorce. I am for people being encouraged to face the strains of marriage with honesty and humility, believing that what God has joined together he is able to help to grow.

But Jesus did say that adultery was a ground for divorce. And I can understand why. If sexual intercourse is the sacrament of marriage, as I said earlier in this book, then to have sexual intercourse with anyone other than your partner is to throw the sacrament away and with it most likely the marriage. I do not believe that adultery need necessarily smash the marriage, but the chances are very high that it will.

Opposing easy divorce and advising against adultery are not the ramblings of an out-of-date, puritanical old fuddy-duddy. It comes from one who knows that for both partners to work at the problems that could lead to divorce, and to turn away from adultery, leaves the way open to what could be for both a final destination of perfect love and with that love a very deep fulfilment.

But the cowards who are afraid of the struggle will bleat away at me for being unrealistic. The truth is that had my wife and I listened to what many well-meaning advisers recommended, and gone ahead and got a divorce, then we would have never known the depth of love and trust that we know today. Those advisers could have robbed us of what for us now is a relationship precious beyond price.

And one last word of bitter warning. I notice on looking back that those people who were so adamant that our marriage could never work, who said that we were incompatible and would always remain so, were in every case people who on closer observation also had marriages that didn't work and were inviting us to join their club. Who are the blind leading the blind? Those who advised us to smash our marriage, or we who, in spite of what seemed intolerable problems, refused to follow their advice, walked into the middle of the pain that was causing the problems, and have come out now on the other side? Thank God, we did not act on their advice.

CHAPTER 20

Growing Old, Dying and Death

I am 56. That must seem young at a time when people generally are living longer than ever. Even so, I am beginning to feel my age. I stopped playing football when I was 40. I played cricket a few times last year but I don't think I shall again. I used to wonder what I would do when my football and cricketing days were over. What would I do for pleasure? Now that those days are gone I find that I don't miss them. I afford myself the luxury of saying the game isn't as good as it was in my day. I have found though that there are compensations. More time to read, to write and to talk with people. I enjoy a certain amount of aloneness, something I never thought I would be able to do.

I may have been more unfortunate than most in that several very good friends of many years' standing have died in recent years, men and women of my own age. I find that making new friends of that quality is difficult, so that old friends of long standing don't get replaced easily. I haven't made many new friends of that kind for quite a long time. So in one sense life is slowly emptying. The plug is out and the water disappearing, and the taps don't work well to replace what is going.

I can understand how the older one gets the emptier of real friends life becomes. But I am not disturbed. I see it as a challenge to face aloneness, not to be dependent on other people for distraction, but instead to find fulfilment in being my age and not living off the youth of younger people.

I suppose that when one has reached the 80s there are very few friends left, and I can understand that if you haven't found the contentment of aloneness by then, life could be miserably lonely. For four years now I have had to spend a lot of time alone. The first enemy that has to be acknowledged and defeated is self-pity. The next is bitterness. The first enforces the cry, 'No one loves me or cares'. The second produces the cry, 'After all I did for them, they now leave me like this'. We must see those cries for the destructive things they are. Destructive of your peace of mind and guilt-making for those at whom these cries are aimed. It is a nasty business.

Aloneness is all right if you walk into it with courage, and doubly all right if you are fortunate enough to be able to relate to a living Jesus.

One day the scientists may be able to double our life span, but those of us today who are heading for the 60s or 70s or 80s won't be here when that happens. We have to face the fact that life is ebbing away fast. We can be miserably lonely as the years tick by, or we can find a strange peace in not having to hurry, in not having to scrabble in the rat race of worldly ambition. There is room to stand back from all the rush and busy-ness, and quietly observe. To learn what Jesus meant when he said that laying up treasure in this world was a waste of time, and that only those things that last for ever are worth working for. I didn't act on that in my forties, but I act on it much more now.

Growing older, when the years between you and death are fewer than those between you and your birth, can be a blessed period. But not for those whose investment is in what 'moth or rust or decay' can attack. For them it must be a growing nightmare.

'Where does your heart lie?' asked Jesus. If your heart belongs only to this world and this life, then you will find that increasing years bring increasing fears. But if your heart rests in those things that belong to eternity, then you can look ahead to visions of greater joy and deeper peace and release from the clamouring demands of the ego.

I cannot say a lot about the process of actually dying, because by its nature I can only relate what I know from second hand, but I have been with many people up to the last hours of life. I can report that when the end is very near the fear dissolves. It is odd that most people spend their lives afraid of dying, but when the time comes to die there is no fear. I have watched so many people die with dignity.

If I have one complaint to make against the Creator it is that dying can be a very messy business. There are some forms of death that have no beauty about them. The ravaged face, the wasted or bloated body, the gasping for breath. None of it is pleasant to observe. And yet most people die with a great dignity of spirit, in spite of the obscenities that happen to the body.

I heard one hospital doctor say (2 May 1977) that in hospital the dying are not treated as people. The human touch in the nursing is missing. The fact that death is imminent is withheld from the patients, and they are not helped to prepare for it. There is a conspiracy of silence.

I remember visiting an old clergyman in Liverpool. When I arrived several of his relatives were in the sitting-room, including his wife and grown-up children. They told me that the old man was dying but that I mustn't tell him this or say anything that might lead him to think he was. When I was alone with him he whispered, 'Roy, old friend, I'm a gonner. I shan't last for much longer, I'm on the way out – but don't tell them downstairs.' What a nonsense. They knew and he knew, but the charade between them was played out to the end.

Unless my own death is sudden I shall want to know if death is at hand, and I shall want to share that with those I love the most, always provided that it wouldn't be cruel to do so. Those with whom I have shared the deepest experiences of life are people with whom I would like to share the deepest experience of all.

I believe with all my heart that Jesus conquered death. I believe that the ultimate purpose of the creation is good. Because I know now that I am held in the everlasting arms, I know that those arms will carry me out beyond death into a life that is beyond my imagination in terms of its beauty, peace, love and truth. To die with dignity not knowing that is very courageous, and it has been done many times, but it is unnecessary. Jesus is here to be known now and can be known to be with us at the hour of our dying.

So we die. All of us. The one fact that we can all be sure of is that this will happen, unless before then Jesus returns to wrap up human history on this planet.

We do not know what lies beyond death in spite of what the spiritualists tell us. Knowing that I enjoy a game of golf, one spiritualist told me that the golf courses in the next life were infinitely better than the ones here! Thoughts of the Americans winning all the golf trophies in heaven as they do on earth wouldn't help me to anticipate heaven with much pleasure. As for the Welsh winning at Rugby for the whole of eternity, well . . . the mind boggles!

Of course, the spiritualists don't know anything about heaven or the after-life. All we know is what Jesus told us: 'I am going to prepare a place for you that where I am there you will be also'. I want a heaven that will be his heaven. He has known what has been best for me in this life, therefore I am content with what he will provide in the next. More than content, I am overjoyed at the thought that it is his world that I shall be entering.

It is the parting that I shall hate. Although my brother died 33 years ago I still miss him. I guess there will be one or two or three people who will shed a tear when I go. The waiting here, for those people whose most treasured loved ones have gone on, is not easy.

The burden of grief and the pain of separation can be eased. Eased by the knowledge that all of our lives are in the loving hands of God. Eased also by learning here and now that although loneliness can bruise the human spirit deeply, aloneness need hold no terrors. I can speak with total authority about this. I have climbed out of the black pit of loneliness into the green pastures of aloneness. I am not particularly courageous, and if I can face aloneness and find that it is not destructive but life-enhancing, so can you. But remember, I never lost my hold on Jesus. Some people say that Christians use the idea of Jesus to take the edge off loneliness. They imply that he isn't really here and that if he is, it is weakness to admit your need for him. They are utterly wrong. He is here. This is not knowledge of the usual kind. I cannot prove it to anyone in the way that I can prove that rain is wet. It is another kind of knowledge. It is knowledge that wells up from the deepest depths of my being, but it is knowledge for all that. I do not claim to know there is God in the way that atheists claim that there is not. I do not arrive at knowing God through a process of logic, although I believe my knowledge is reasonable. Knowledge of God does not come through logic but through faith and experience.

Is it so wrong to admit a need for him? He said he had come for those who felt lost. He said that the good shepherd went up the mountains to rescue the lost sheep. And furthermore I am not ashamed to admit that I do need him. I know from experience how horribly wrong life can go without him.

If you want to argue that what I am saying is the babbling of a weak, frightened idiot, then I'm afraid you will be saying that on your own. I won't be listening. My faith and knowledge of Jesus has been tested at a very deep level and I have the sublime arrogance to say to anyone who accuses me of being a weak-minded, neurotic lump, 'You are wrong'. My love for him and my knowledge of him are the sanest aspects of my being.

So we can live with the knowledge of our certain death, as a friendly companion. Not as a hideous monster from whom we must flee. I shall welcome death when it comes, and I shall pray that those who may be hurt by my going will find that without my presence they will not be destroyed.

CHAPTER 21

Solitude — A First Look

I hope that by now you understand what I mean by loneliness, and that you understand what I mean when I say that loneliness is bad. God never intended us to face loneliness.

I hope also that you understand what I mean by facing aloneness, which is a good, enriching experience that can enhance every other relationship that we may have.

Now, I must ask, what is meant by Solitude? It could be misunderstood as loneliness, but it is not that. It could be misunderstood as having arrived at the position of being able to stand alone, without need, without dependency. It is not that either. Solitude is way beyond loneliness and beyond aloneness. It is something special, something that exists within its own right.

What is it?

I can describe easily what it is not. It is not enforced loneliness. It is not hanging on by your eyebrows and being able to be alone.

Solitude is pure, undiluted joy. It was what Jesus went to find when he left everybody and went on his own to be alone. He was not saying, 'Poor old me, nobody wants me'. He was not saying, 'I am alone and that is good'. He was looking for something else. It has to do with being alone with God, with being at one with the universe.

When I was young I used to look at the night sky, imagining how vast the universe is. That didn't make me feel lonely but it did make me feel very small and of no consequence. The size of the universe never frightened me; all I felt was how magnificent it all was and how insignificant I was.

One day I was walking along a suburban road which was lined with trees. On either side of the road were pleasant middle-class houses. It wasn't a busy road but it was an occupied road. As I walked along I felt this great upsurge of joy. I felt that my head was going to burst. Can you guess what I did? I stopped at the next tree, threw my arms around it and loved it. And the tree loved me. Mad? Of course I was mad. Yet in that moment, that precious, never-to-be-forgotten moment, I knew that I belonged. Completely alone with a tree, and yet I belonged to the whole vast universe. I was not living in a universe that was alien to me or I to it. I was part of the whole thing. Apart from the tree I was alone when it happened, but I wasn't alone, I belonged. Solitude is not being alone, or lonely, it is knowing that you belong to the whole of creation.

Why is it, I wonder, that science fiction almost always presents 'beings' from outer space as our antagonists? The Daleks of 'Dr Who' can only say, 'Exterminate, exterminate all members of the human race'. When the scriptwriters for TV or films depict 'beings' from other planets or outer space, they are almost always shown as alien to us, as wanting to destroy us. Why do they do this? On what evidence do they assume this? What evidence we do have does not corroborate that idea.

We have been to the moon. We wouldn't want to live there, but the moon did not destroy the human beings who landed on it. We have landed a probe on Mars and no terrible monster arrived to smash our probe to pieces. From what we have learned so far, the universe is not determined to annihilate us. We couldn't live on those two planets for long because we have been made to live on the planet Earth, but the two planets where we have landed something haven't indicated that we don't belong to the universe and that we must be exterminated.

I don't know whether or not there are 'beings' on other planets. People like Patrick Moore of TV's 'The Sky at Night' fame, are sure that somewhere in the universe there must be other planets where the climatic and atmospheric conditions are suitable for life to exist and for 'beings' to exist. Patrick Moore is a knowledgeable astronomer but

I do have the temerity to question whether or not he is right.

The universe is immense and we know that there are billions and billions of galaxies, and each one has millions and millions of stars, and each star has several planets, so surely, Patrick Moore and others say, there must be other intelligent beings on some of them. Well, there may be, but on the other hand there may not be. This planet Earth could be unique. Unique in the vast, fathomless, infinity of the universe. What evidence we have got, which is minute, confirms that so far as we know we are the only beings that exist. I dismiss UFOs (unidentified flying objects) as calculated phonies or the false impressions of otherwise sane and honest people.

As far as we know, actually know, we are the only beings that exist in the universe. We can guess or calculate from all the probabilities that there must be other beings in outer space, but we don't know there are.

Lurking about in the minds of people who believe in beings from outer space may be the dreadful fear that as a planet ours may be unique. Following from that is the thought that Patrick Moore may be unique. He looks it, bless him!

What I am saying is that just as every human being is unique, so our planet may be unique. One thing I have learned is that as you look outward into space and it becomes increasingly mysterious, so as you look inward into the molecule and then into the atom, that also becomes increasingly mysterious. We seem to be standing in between two worlds. One that is outward that defies our comprehension, and one that looks inwards that is equally vast and beyond our means of understanding. My belief is that we humans stand in the known observing two unknowns. If we look outward we are baffled, and if we look inward we are equally at a loss to understand.

Is it because we are afraid of being alone that we need to believe that there are other beings in outer space?

There are some people who, feeling this awful dilemma of being alive in a universe that they cannot understand, a universe that contains so much mystery, turn to spiritualism as a solace. It is not enough to be who they are, relating to other living human beings on this planet, they must make contact with those who have died whom they believe can still contact us. It is one way of feeling less lonely. The only trouble is that a lot of spiritualism is nonsense.

I have been told by several different people that they have made contact with someone whom they love who has died. The intermediary has been a Red Indian spirit guide. A Red Indian! Why an Indian, and why Red? And what are the incredible messages that their loved one has passed on to them through their Red Indian spirit guide? One person told me, actually told me, that the message was, 'Kick the hot water bottle out of bed'! The mind boggles and so it should.

A friend of mine, Dr Donald J. West, a psychiatrist, was employed by the Society of Psychical Research to investigate psychical phenomena. He said that a lot of what went on at seances was sheer trickery. For instance, ectoplasm – that is the stuff that comes out of the medium's mouth and forms into the shape of your lost loved one. The only snag was that when photographed and enlarged one photograph showed quite clearly the name of the manufacturer of the butter muslin that was being used. If I understand Donald correctly, most of what is claimed to be evidence of an 'after-life' is either fraud or can be explained in perfectly normal ways.

I have never been to a seance but I have been to many spiritualist services in spiritualist churches. The 'messages' that were given were as useless as the messages given by astrologers in all the popular papers and magazines.

I could earn a fortune if only some national newspaper would employ me to do it. I could tell you what the 'spirits' say and the 'stars foretell'. For instance, 'You are going to get a surprise'. Well, who isn't? Or, 'You will be going on a journey'. Well, who won't, even if it is only two bus stops away? 'Now is the time to be careful with your money.' I don't know about you, but I'm always worried about money!

I don't need the 'stars' or 'spirits' to give me that kind of message.

There are, however, more sophisticated kinds of 'messages'. I could learn a lot about you by the look on your face, the way you sit in your chair, what you do with your hands, or legs or knees or ears. I could learn a lot about you from the messages that your body is giving out, provided I am observant enough. There is a lot I could learn about you even though I haven't made enquiries about you before I meet you, although I believe that some fortune-tellers do.

I am not saying that the people who give you these kinds of 'messages' are not useful. They may be telling you something about yourself that previously you hadn't realized. But to persuade you that 'spirits' or the 'stars' were telling them about you is, for me, absolute bunk.

All this kind of thing is an escape that some people use for backing away from solitude.

At spiritualistic church services I have observed the most utterly lonely people of all. It was dreadfully sad to see them. At all costs they are not going to feel lonely. At all costs they are not going to search for what aloneness is really all about. And even in a thousand years they are going to run like mad from solitude. I do not condemn them. Their sadness made me want to weep. To go to such places because you have lost the one person who had made your life worth while would indicate to me that you haven't found out who you are. Or so it seemed. I couldn't judge them, or condemn or even criticize them. Even writing this makes me feel like a heel, trying to take away the only comfort that they have left. 'Maybe the medium will have a message from the beyond for me tonight.' Maybe the 'stars' are telling me something. Who am I to try and persuade these people that it is all rubbish? I only have the right to say that if I can offer them something better in return.

I believe that what they are dabbling in could be dangerous. One bishop told me that spiritualism is the only way that people today could be helped to believe in an 'after-life'. He was very angry when I disagreed and he reported me to my superiors. Of course there are mysteries about the powers of the human mind, but I won't, and nor should you, settle for what appears to be ready-made answers. There may be telepathy. There may be interconnection based on extra-sensory perception between people alive on this planet now, and even between people on this planet and people who have 'died'. I don't know that there is. I would rather live with what I know than with what may be the truth.

I know that Jesus lived. I know that Jesus died. I know that Jesus rose from the dead. Do you understand what I mean when I say that is all I need to know?

What then about this solitude business?

Solitude has nothing at all to do with spiritualism or astrology or some eastern cults that go in for what is called meditation. I really am staggered by what some people fall for. There are those who will tell you that if you can find the right mantra and keep on repeating it minute after minute, hour after hour, day after day (what you do for a living is anyone's guess), then you will find peace of mind and total serenity. Stand on Oxford Circus tube station in London and look at the ad. for this kind of absurdity and you could be persuaded to think that by saying 'Hari krishna, Hari krishna, Krishna Murti, Krishna Hari, Hari Krishna' and so on, over and over again, then you will get peace of mind. After a long day's work in London, tired, and longing to get home, you feel so exhausted and empty of resources that standing on the station waiting for the tube, worried stiff about your family, your job and your overdraft, you could be persuaded that to say that garble over and over again might help. You are, at that point, reduced to thinking that anything might help!

I've done it. For many years I stood on that tube platform and looked at the picture of a very fat man implying that if I repeated a mantra over and over again then some kind of peace of mind would come to me. What nonsense! Mind you, the other advertising posters weren't much better. There you are, tired, exhausted and you have worked hard all day for your family, and some idiot has planned for you to look at a poster which says, 'Do you really care for your family?' or words to that effect, and then goes on to say, 'Why don't you join our insurance scheme, or invest your money in us?' 'What money?' I used to ask. But they had got me where it really hurt. I do love my family and to be asked if I was doing enough for them could only receive the weak, quivering answer of the man reading it saying, 'No, I don't do enough'. What else could he do except jump in front of the train?

That is just one glimpse into the rat race that we call being civilized.

Against that terribly noisy, pushing and shoving, trampling on other people, striving at all costs to provide for your family 'world', I have stood. I have stood on that tube platform and been shoved and pushed and bellowed at by the posters, and heard the seductive voices of some of the posters asking, 'Do you really love your family?', and have said weakly, 'Yes', and they have said, 'Do this, do that', and you know that you can't do it and you arrive home feeling a totally washed out failure. Do you wonder that some men turn to drink? Are you surprised that some loving wives can't understand that when their man arrives home he is utterly spent and exhausted, and the thought of more activity in bed is quite beyond him?

In spite of all that dare I mention the value of solitude? I haven't even mentioned the problems of the mother at home with a house to keep tidy, shopping to be done, meals to prepare, children to keep occupied, washing and ironing, and then a husband who will arrive home hoping to be loved and cared for.

Dare I mention solitude to the person who, after a day's work and all the shoving and pushing to get home, arrives and there is nobody there because he lives on his own?

Or the person who has worked all day on his own, in a field or a factory (where the noise of the machines makes human communication impossible)?

Or the homosexual who has been isolated all day in his own world and goes home at night to nothing, because 'something' would be condemned by the world?

Believe me, my friend, I know what it is like, and my wife knows what it is like, to feel alone even when together. Bodily you may be together, or you may not be, but as far as you, the essential you, is concerned you could still be alone.

You have gone a great distance if you have battled through loneliness and shed the misery of self-pity. You have achieved great heights if you have found aloneness and are happy and content to live within that.

What though about solitude? What has that got to offer? If that offers nothing then we might as well stay as we are or turn to spiritualism, astrology, palmistry, phrenology, mantras and the rest to find our peace, our wholeness, our serenity, our sanity.

CHAPTER 22

Solitude — What It Is

Solitude is not loneliness. Nor is it simply being able to stand alone. It is something else.

Jesus must have been tempted to feel lonely at times. According to the records no one really understood what he was on about until after he died. His family thought that he was mad. His closest friends followed him, not because they really understood him but because they thought they did, but they had got it wrong. Sometimes he almost lost his patience with their inability to see the meaning of his words and deeds.

Because of this he went on into the experience of being alone. He had to stand alone even amongst the vast crowds who followed him. One gets the impression that frequently he went up into the hills on his own to be alone with God. He seemed to draw great strength from those times.

Was he doing that to reaffirm his belief that he did really belong to the universe? His experience amongst his friends, his enemies, and the crowds was tending to persuade him that he didn't belong. Alone in the hills he knew that he did. He was at one with the whole of creation. He was at one with mankind, although mankind wasn't at one with him. He could identify with every human being he met. He could get inside their skin or, as the Bible says, 'He could see right into the heart of man'.

There can come times when for us the misery and pain of loneliness can change into the peace and contentment of aloneness. I know plenty of people who live alone and are quite happy. I know others who enjoy being in company but who also enjoy being alone without fear.

Solitude, though, is an experience beyond aloneness. It is more than peace and contentment because it includes joy. Many people think that joy means being very happy.

It doesn't. Happiness is when things are going well for you. Happiness is when an expected tragedy doesn't happen. Happiness can mean getting more money so that your financial anxieties are eased. Happiness is when you discover that someone you love also loves you. Happiness can mean getting drunk or becoming 'high' on drugs. Happiness is when your team wins the Cup Final. Happiness can be the reward for a job well done. Happiness can mean seeing your children settled and comfortable.

Joy is something else.

I believe that solitude is the result of being able to stand alone plus the joy of knowing that you belong.

On 3 April 1977 in the *Observer* newspaper, Malcolm Muggeridge described how he feels, now that he is becoming old and knowing that death cannot be far away. He wrote: 'I have a heightened sense of the beauty of our earth, its shapes and smells and creatures, and of the delight of human work and human love, as well as a confidence past stating, that as an infinitesimal particle of creation myself, I am a participant in the Creator's purposes.'

I believe him. I was visiting him and Kitty, his wife, at a time when I was writing a biography of Malcolm. There too was Andrew Boyle, the writer, who also created that extremely good radio programme, 'The World at One'. In those days (the early 70s) it was Malcolm's routine to work in the mornings and the evenings, and to walk in the afternoons. I know this from personal, footsore experience. On my first visit, dressed as for the BBC in London, I was very quickly handed a thick sweater and a pair of gum-boots and off we went, Malcolm, Kitty, Andrew and I. It was one of those walks when without any conscious thought you change partners from time to time. When I was walking with Malcolm it was quite obvious that he was exhilarated by the natural world around him. He simply revelled in it, his quick eye picking up details and commenting upon them. Yet he had been born, and grew up, in Croydon. He had lived and worked in London, Manchester, Moscow, Washington, Delhi, Calcutta. Here was no countryman from experience, but here was a man who loved creation and he was one with it. I believe that he hates man-made towns and cities, and feels like an alien when he is in them. Where he belongs is in the God-made creation around us. Even in cities he looks for what is God-made and revels in it, but what is man-made gives him little delight.

As I walked along with him that day (or rather, plodded) the thought kept occurring to me that he was a 'loner', a man who knew the ecstasies of solitude and enjoyed them to the full. And yet he is the most stimulating companion that you could wish for, one of those rare people who makes whoever is with him feel that they are the most important person in his life at that moment. It is an uncommon gift. How different are bishops' garden parties, and other such-like jamborees, when whoever you are talking with is looking past your head for someone more important than you whom they would prefer to be with. In my case I am never surprised that they should do this, for at all such functions I feel that everyone else present is more important, and much more interesting to talk with than me. It hurts a little to feel it, but it seems just.

Malcolm Muggeridge, then, a man of the town who loves nature. A wonderful companion who revels in solitude. A man who has known the abject miseries of loneliness but who is able when necessary to stand alone with courage.

I asked a seventeen-year-old girl to describe to me today what solitude was all about. All she could think of was that it would be like some solitary confinement. I know that there have been some brave souls who have experienced solitude even when locked up in a cell in solitary confinement. One such is Canon Gonville ffrench Beytagh. He was put into solitary confinement in Johannesburg for protesting against the treatment of political prisoners. I asked him how he had survived without going mad. He told me that at first he only had three material things, his cell, his bed and a receptacle for bodily functions. Then he found under the bed two bristles from a broom. He bent them into the shape of a cross. Then he went on to tell me that what kept him calm and sane was a deepening awareness that although he was alone at the same time he belonged, and it was this sense of belonging that changed his period of solitary confinement into an experience of solitude. He said that he began to feel that he was not on his own, but that he belonged to the whole Christian family on earth and in heaven. 'Therefore,' says the C. of E. Prayer Book, 'with Angels and Archangels and with all the company of heaven we laud and magnify thy glorious Name'.

We belong! All of us! Although at times we may feel we are isolated, we can all be participants in the Creator's purposes. I can understand someone who doesn't believe in a Creator feeling separated off from the human race and from the universe. The universe for them can only be a vast collection of parts that don't belong to each other. They say that I am a separate part, so are you, so is the mountain, so is the earth, so is the moon and all the stars, they are all just parts that don't belong to each other. If there is a Creator and he is good then all the parts should be able to come together to form a whole. I am only a tiny part, says Malcolm Muggeridge, but 'I have a confidence,' he says, that 'I am a participant in the Creator's purposes'. Albert Einstein believed that all the parts belong, that behind this wonderfully designed universe was an intelligence before which we could only stand in awe.

I believe that it is within solitude that we can find the confidence that we belong, and out of that there comes the experience of indescribable joy. Not belonging because I am tied to anything or anybody, not belonging because your colour is the same as mine, or we speak the same language, not belonging because we always agree or wear the same sized shoes. I belong to every blade of grass, every star, every person, every tree, every animal, every flower. It is within solitude that I find this, everything and everybody belonging because we all belong to God as revealed in Jesus. 'Underneath,' says the Bible, 'are the everlasting arms.' Everything is held together by those 'arms'.

There is, however, a destructive power at work, the power of evil. That power is disruptive. That power, which I will call the devil, seeks to divide and separate. He seeks to separate man from God, to separate men and women from mankind, and to separate mankind from nature and the rest of creation.

It is the devil who causes loneliness, the devil working in me and working in you to keep us apart. It is the devil who whispers in my ear, 'You don't belong, hate them for excluding you', or he whispers, 'They are different from you, hate them for it and destroy them'. Or he says, 'They have got what you want, kill them and take it from them'.

In the Bible, in the letter to the Hebrews chapter 12 verse one, it reads: 'Therefore, since we are surrounded by so great a cloud of witnesses, let us lay aside every weight, and sin which clings so closely, and let us run with perseverance the race that is set before us, looking to Jesus the pioneer and perfector of our faith, who for the joy that was set before him endured the cross, despising the shame, and is seated at the right hand of the throne of God' (RSV).

We are surrounded by 'a great cloud of witnesses', we belong. Let us lay aside everything that ties us to this world. He endured the cross because of the joy that was set before him. What was he 'enduring on the cross'? Physical pain all right. A Roman crucifixion and the flogging that preceded it was absolute physical agony. There wasn't a single human being alive then who understood what was happening within him as he hung on that cross. He was alone. His own integrity was holding him to that cross. He had the power to leave that blackness of pain and mental torture. He was choosing to be where he was. Then something happened that we who are only human will never be able to experience or fully understand. He felt separated from God. Jesus, the Son of God, Jesus who was one with the Creator when creation began, Jesus who had said, 'I and the Father are one. He who has seen me has seen the Father,' was split away from the Father. His aloneness was total. This was the moment when as a free, completely independent person he could have saved his own life. He could have denied the existence of God. He could have reviled the human race who had put him on that cross. And if he had done that then the devil would have won. The devil and evil and sin, which at that moment had come between Jesus and the Father, would have triumphed and human beings would for ever after have been in the devil's power. For ever we would have been separated from one another, from creation, and from God.

That is not what happened. Jesus did not come down from the cross. He did not condemn humanity. He did not curse the Father who seemed to have deserted him. He stayed where he was. Somehow, and I for one do not know how he did it, somehow he went into the deepest, darkest depths of aloneness that it is possible for a person to go. Deeper than anyone other than he could go. And he was not defeated.

Why did he do it? He, who appeared not to belong. He, who was totally rejected. He, who drank the cup of loneliness and aloneness to its deepest and bitterest dregs, why, why did he do it?

Because he knew that if he did, then there was joy ahead, not just for himself but for the whole human race. The Bible says, and I repeat it, he endured everything that happened on that cross because of the joy that would be made possible for everyone.

What is that joy? It is the joy of knowing that there is nothing that can separate us from one another, from creation, from God, if we can take into ourselves the victory that he won for us. I don't think that any of those states of being are possible without him.

Loneliness is a nightmare without him, and without him I doubt if we can enter the loneliness of another human being and help them to know that they belong. Without him what can they belong to? There is nothing and no one else that is permanent. How can you, the insignificant, infinitesimal you stand against a universe that seems alien to you, and declare I am? The universe could crush you into non-existence more easily than you could crush a flea.

As for solitude, the joy of knowing that you belong to mankind, to creation, to God, that would never have been known without him.

I remember, not all that long ago, lying in a bed in a room of a mental hospital. It was a National Health hospital, but I was in a room on my own. I was in total despair. Not only was I on my own but I felt that there was no one outside that room who cared a damn. I know now that there were some who did care. But that night, on my own, I did not know. I was totally and completely alone. I was not just separated from other human beings, I felt that my selfhood had no meaning within the universe.

Then the door opened. There was no light on in the room. I was in total darkness. Someone came in and sat by my bed. I asked him who he was. He said that he was a visiting psychiatrist, and that he had asked for permission to observe me. I had been warned that this might happen and I had been asked if I had any objections. I had said that I had no objection, but by the time this man came in I had forgotten all this. His entry came as a complete surprise.

There I was, alone, on my own, in the depths of despair. Out of the darkness, right by my bed, came this reassuring voice asking, 'How are you feeling?' I said, 'Dreadful'. 'Why?' the voice asked. I told him, 'There is no meaning to life. There is no purpose in being a human being. There is no life after death. I cannot see a single glimmer of hope. Why should I go on living? Do you think that there is any final ultimate purpose in continuing as a human being?' I asked. The voice answered, 'No!' and went on, 'All you can hope for is finding pleasure here and now'. Here and now? Who was this crazy idiot who was saying that? A bit of pleasure here and now when I was contemplating suicide here and now. After a while he left. I never found out who he was, what his name was, where he had come from nor where he is now.

If that wasn't the devil, then I hope I never hear the voice of anyone who is.

What would you have done then?

I'll tell you what I did and have continued to do. I know

that Jesus defeated all the 'powers' that say that human life is meaningless, that the earth is a nonsense in a universe that makes no sense. Jesus makes the whole universe make sense. He has made it possible for people like you and me to say 'I belong'. That night in the mental hospital bed I had to decide who I believed; to which wagon I would hitch my star. Was that visiting voice in the dark telling me the truth, or was it Jesus hanging on that cross who was telling me the truth? I decided for Jesus. It might have been perverse; but a middle-class voice, that sounded as though he was wearing a middle-class suit, didn't carry the same conviction as a man who had no clothes, was a carpenter, roughed it with a bunch of drop-outs, who was loved and respected by prostitutes and other dodgy characters, and who went through what he went through in order that people like you and me should know that we do belong. I chose Jesus. That decision didn't alter the feelings of despair, but it did deepen my resolve to go on being a Jesus person. I had been offered a completely free choice. I made my choice. Choosing Jesus did not give me any advantage in this world, nor when I come to think of it did it give me any advantage in the next one, because going on living after death was not what the question was all about. The question was, 'Is there any meaning in being alive now?' The voice in the dark said, 'There is no meaning,' and Jesus on the cross said, 'There is,' and Malcolm Muggeridge says, 'I have confidence that cannot be stated that I am a participant in the Creator's purpose.'

As the old saying has it: 'You pays your money and you takes your choice'.

I have made my choice.

Solitude is when everyone around you is saying, 'You are nothing, your life is meaningless, the universe rejects you', and you are able to say, 'My life is not meaningless and nor is the selfhood of any other human being'. Solitude for me is knowing that life is not without meaning. I may get lost on the way, but there is no reason why I should stay lost.

I have experienced those moments when I have known

that I belonged to every blade of grass, to every twig on every tree, to every bird, to every fish, to every worm, to every grain of soil in every field, to every grain of sand on every beach. I belong. It has been in solitude that I have found this.

I am not worthy to belong. I am a dreadful old sinner in a thousand different ways. Yet, if I can think that I, miserable, depressed, panic-ridden no-good that I sometimes feel I am, can belong, then my dear friend, I know that you belong. You can experience that bliss of solitude, of knowing that you belong. To hell (and I mean that) with the devil, who wants to persuade us that we don't belong. Let us enter the joy that Jesus made possible, that we do belong.

All my instincts tell me that there is a choice lurking about here. The arguments one way or another cancel each other out. The psychiatrist whispered into my ear, 'Your life has no meaning,' and Jesus hanging on a cross says, 'Your life has got meaning'. The choice was mine. The choice is yours.

Out of my choice I found solitude. Those rare moments when I know that I belong. A choice that I couldn't have made if Jesus hadn't made the choice that he made.

> 'Jesus, I thank you for making it possible for me to make the choice I did. I thank you that even though I am the no-good person that I think I am, you love me. You make me feel that I do belong. You made that possible when you died for me. Whoever is reading what I am writing now, may they also feel and know that they belong and that in solitude they may find that this is the truth.'

Chapter 23

Are Christians Perfect?

The answer is that obviously we are not. The commonest charge against people who go to church is that all who do are hypocrites. And if you are a clergyman as I am, then the standard expected of you is nothing short of the angelic.

Christians come from the common stock of humanity. We are born in exactly the same way as everyone else. We have the same experiences as everyone else in the womb, during the birth trauma and in the first years of our life. Until the moment of our conversion we have the same resources or lack of them common to the whole of humanity. At conversion a new element enters our life, a relationship with Jesus and through him with God. Our moral standards change, our values change, our objectives change. In order to move towards these new goals we have access to a source of help that comes to us through what Jesus accomplished for us. There is a new life force within us that we call the activity of the Holy Spirit. We are 'born again' in the sense that we begin to shed the pseudo-self that 'the world' has induced us to be, and we begin to come to terms with who we really are, namely the self that God created.

But shedding the old and adopting completely the new is a long, hard struggle, and this is a struggle that will not be completed this side of the grave. So there are Christians at different stages of development. On accepting one's position as a Christian all the problems that one had before do not disappear overnight. As the New Testament says, at the start of the Christian life we are babies, living along with an old, well entrenched pseudo-self (the 'old man' of the New Testament). Christian growth is the growth of the baby Christian and the slow destruction of the 'old man'. But this process takes time.

It is not therefore surprising that some Christians are still prone to anxiety, feel pangs of deep loneliness, can't get their sex life right, still need the help of psychiatrists, suffer from agoraphobia, claustrophobia (and any other of the 57 phobias that exist). Christians can still be short-tempered, jealous, selfish, dominating, possessive, power-hungry and even have to go into mental hospital as I did.

What matters is that we are growing out of the old into the new. 'Behold I am *making* all things new,' said Jesus, and that implies a process. There are some problems that a Christian may have now that will not be completely resolved in this life. But no matter. The growth is taking place, the transformation is happening.

Some Christians get into a lather of guilt because they are not yet perfect. It is important to realize that some of our troubles are not our own fault. If you were knocked down by a car driven by a drunken driver and you had to have a leg amputated, you would never think of blaming yourself and feeling guilty because you had lost a leg. If as a child you needed love and love wasn't forthcoming, or you needed food and the supply was inadequate, or you needed company but were left for hour upon hour lying helpless in a cot suffering the terrible misery of feeling completely abandoned, then you cannot blame yourself if in later life you have neurotic symptoms that result from what has happened.

If you did not have a free-flowing, happy relationship with your parents when you were a child, it is likely that you will not find it easy to develop trusting relationships later on. In one way or another we have all been conditioned by our early years. The outside world in which we grew up will have added to that conditioning. When we arrive at the point where our new Christian life begins all that conditioning is still there and it has to be undone, and again I say this will take time.

However, not all of our troubles are the result of what has been done to us. Some of our troubles result from choices that we made before we were Christians, choices that we made out of weakness or fear or straightforward sinfulness. It takes courage to relate honestly with other people, and often we did not have the courage. We acted in ways that we knew were wrong, ways in which we need not have acted but we did. All this is part of the 'old man' in us. Patterns of behaviour that we chose and went on choosing are still there when our Christian life begins. All this too has to be undone.

But it is not only a matter of tangles from the past having to be undone. In the Christian a new life has emerged, and as that new life emerges the old life will slowly be pushed out of its position of dominance.

The Christian is a person who has hope. The present situation is not beyond salvation. No matter what the results of the past may be, they can all be dealt with. Some of those results will be taken completely away. Others which cannot be taken away can be grappled with and kept under control. The past does not have to decide the present.

However I must now issue a stern word of warning to those people who are Christians, quite apart from those who are not. I am as certain as I am about anything, that Jesus Christ is alive now. We may go through periods of loneliness as far as human companionship is concerned, but when all human companionship has failed our relationship with Jesus remains intact. But we are tempted not to capitalize on this. I know that there have been times when I did not do that. Because human relationships failed I was tempted to include Jesus in them. What a mistake that would have been! The whole point about Jesus Christ is that when human beings collapse, he does not, because he was not and is not only human. He is the one who can relate to me as a human being, but also relate to me as the divine Son of God. This is not just a hope. Where I have been, you don't simply cling to hopes, you need something that is rock hard and steady. So, when human relationships failed me, there he was, utterly real and true. This is not an escape from loneliness, it is the answer to it.

If it were not so I would not try to deceive you.

So, standing out of your loneliness there is him. This is part of the 'Good News' – the Gospel.

So, and it has to be said, when people contemplate suicide (as I have done) this simply spells out that the living relationship with Jesus that is possible is not as real as it needs to be. This is not a criticism of those who go that way. Who am I to judge them? But can we, you and I, when we come to that moment that feels like total abandonment, still go on trusting in him? It all depends on what you have been doing until that moment comes. Do you regularly turn to him in trust and address yourself to him? If you have done this, then when the darkness comes (as surely it will) you will not be alone. You may be praying to him out of the dark, to a Jesus that you are not sure is there, but you will go on praying. And from my experience of having walked that way, if you persist in relating to him, then the clouds do roll away eventually and the sunshine breaks through. But it is a hard road to travel, and many give up because they lack the courage to go on trusting that what they believe in their innermost hearts is true.

It is the silence, however, that bothers me. Not the silence between us and Jesus, but the silence between us and others. Why does the suicide take us by complete surprise? Why did that person live in the depths of loneliness and feel that he could not communicate his worst thoughts and feelings to another human being? He or she must feel that we are not to be trusted. How far can people trust us with their worst feelings of self-loathing? Which is another way of saying, how far will our love go?

On many occasions I have said to audiences or congregations, 'Here we are, and every one of us is neurotic'. And I have been met with surprise, shock, sheer unbelief. Yet that is the truth. There is not a single human being in the western world who is not neurotic to a greater or lesser extent. If only we would all realize this, then we would be far less condemning of those who are acting from their own neurotic drives. However, because we will not accept that we too are neurotic we back away from anyone else who displays their own particular neurosis to us. So we all play this stupid game of pretending with each other, each of us imagining that we are completely balanced and normal human beings. As I have said before, there is no such person as the perfectly balanced unneurotic person. No wonder that Jesus said, 'Judge not lest you be judged'. But we go on doing so in spite of what we know is the truth about ourselves. Let us then, with total frankness, own up to someone else whom we trust what the hidden drives are that remain with us, and even if no human being can understand and accept us, we can be certain that Jesus does.

However, what about sin? That is not the same as being driven by neurotic powers. Sin is what we deliberately choose. We may excuse this on the grounds of what has happened to us in our childhood, or of what has happened to us since. But sin is the free choice of doing what we should not have done, or failing to do what we should have done. That is our responsibility.

In the early days of Methodism there was what was called the Class Meeting. I know that there are Methodist Class Meetings today, but they bear no comparison to what they were when Methodism began. In those early years the members of the Class were encouraged to speak out their sins in front of the Class. And in that intimate and trusting environment the word of forgiveness could be spoken. I am not necessarily advocating that we should return to the practice of open confession, but I feel most deeply that there should be people whom we know and trust to whom we can go privately, and openly confess our sins. If we do not, or there is not the provision to do so, then the agony of real guilt will remain within us. Is it not enough, you may ask, to make your confession to Jesus in private? No, it is not. Jesus established the Church to be his body, and each member of his Church has to be his body in one way or the other. So there must be some people whose gift it is to hear what we have to say about our sins, and in the name of Jesus explain that our sins are forgiven provided that the repentance has been genuine.

However, just as our guilt and shame usually remain a private thing, so the nature of sin remains a thing not to be discussed or described. Sin is whatever stands between me and my relationship with God. Who, though, is prepared to make clear what is sin and what is the result of my deep neurotic drives? For this we all need a counsellor, and there are few of them about. Recently a book has been published by the Rev. Kenneth Leech called *Soul Friend*, and in it he has traced with immense scholarship how throughout the whole history of the Christian Church there has been a continuing presence of men and women who have been endowed with the spiritual graces that are required to fill this vitally important function. Not all people can listen to the sins of another without condemnation and abhorrence, but I believe that the Jesus who founded the Church has not left us in this generation without any such people. It is for us to find them, to seek them out, and they will be people whom instinctively we can trust. People who are firmly grounded in the love of Jesus Christ, who can minister to those so desperately in need of the word of forgiveness.

It is not only the gift of listening to the sins that are acknowledged that is required, it is also the gift of being able to make clear where sin exists and where it does not. It is utterly useless to confuse sin with neurosis, and it is equally as damaging to write off sin as though it were only a neurosis. We need people who know the difference and who are able to make clear which is which.

Neurosis cuts us off from mankind, and sin cuts us off from God. Therein lie the real causes of loneliness. The journey into aloneness and then into the bliss of solitude can be managed by some on their own, but my suspicion is that the vast majority of us need a human counsellor who for us can be the mind and words of Jesus Christ himself. Such people do exist, and it is worth taking a lot of trouble to find one.

However, when we look at it, loneliness should not exist. If it does exist then we must face the fact that it is our failure, our collective failure, that we and others are burdened by it.

I offer you my conviction that God Almighty understands that we will experience loneliness, but he has also made provision that it can be banished, and banished for ever.

CHAPTER 24

The Place of Prayer

This book at its heart assumes the central place that Jesus Christ must have in our lives. It assumes what he was, what he did and who he is now. Undergirding and overshadowing everything that I have written is Jesus Christ, to whom we can relate now. Jesus Christ as revealed to us in the New Testament. Jesus Christ with whom here and now we can have a two-way relationship.

Whether we choose him or he chooses us I do not know. That is an argument that has been going on for a very long time, and I have no wish to go into that now. However, it seems to me that without a relationship with him the possibility of unrelenting loneliness is extremely likely, the journey into aloneness is extremely unlikely and the chance of experiencing the bliss of solitude is very remote.

The rock of his presence with us now is the one relationship which will not break down from his side when all other relationships have. He is the one that we can depend on when we feel that it is necessary to stand alone, without the aid or support of any human being. And it is with him that there comes to us that knowledge that we belong to the whole of creation.

All that only becomes possible through the medium of our prayerful relationship with him. Prayer then is vital. It is very difficult, if not impossible, to explain what is happening when we pray, and how it is possible for him to be with us and in what way. And yet more than 99% of all the people I have met have known how to do it when the need has been deep enough. The most unlikely people pray at times. There is no doubt that at most of the funerals I conduct the mourners pray, even though it may have been a long time since they last did. When a close relation or friend is in trouble or danger, people who normally would not pray turn to prayer. What are they doing? Are they reaching out in utter desperation with a blind superstitious hope that maybe, maybe there is something, someone, who can offer some aid when all human help has failed? Is prayer the same kind of thing as carrying a rabbit's foot in your pocket for luck, or wearing a lucky scarf as Battle of Britain pilots did? Is prayer just an act motivated by superstition, that we cling to because the events of life carry such danger, such threat, such menace and seem so powerful that in acknowledging our own human weakness and powerlessness we hope that there is some power beyond ourselves to whom we can turn for help?

It is very odd, if such movements to the more powerful are just superstition with no basis in reality, it is very odd that from the beginnings of man's history he has done this. He may have imagined this power to have been the sun, or a mountain or a river, or the sea or an idol that he had fashioned, but what he could be saying is that deep in the deepest part of the mind of man is the knowledge that there is someone else, someone who transcends the limitations of humanity.

I believe that to be the case. I go along with St Augustine who said that 'God has made us for himself and that our hearts will know no rest till they find their rest in him'. I believe in God, but I find the idea of God too big to grasp. I believe in God but I find it very difficult to relate to the one who created this vast, fathomless universe. Jesus I find is a completely different proposition. Here is someone whom I can know through the pages of the New Testament. Here is someone who had a body like mine, a mind like mine, a nature like mine. Jesus is someone to whom I can relate. And because he was man *and* God, in relating to him I am relating also to the divine. The power I need when all human help has failed I find in him, because he was more than simply a man.

I need this relationship. When I journeyed through that time of my life when I felt completely cut off from all human contact, there was still him. When all conceivable kind of hope in the prospects of happiness, never mind joy, had gone, he was still there and it was he who kept the flickering flame of hope burning. I can testify that when the temptation to sin is clamouring at the doorway of my being and I know that alone I will not be able to resist, I call out 'Help me, Help me', and he does. I fail only at those times when I do not call upon his help, or blatantly refuse the help that he is offering me. It is vital for me that I stay in a close relationship with him. When I sink into chronic depths of depression and want to hide from him, although he does not remove the depression he stays with me as I struggle through it. Even at those times when my mind is too exhausted through strain or stress to concentrate on the fact of his presence, I find that I can still murmur, 'May thy will be done'.

Prayer, however, does not come naturally to me. I have to make a conscious decision to pray. When I do I know that he is there. It is impossible to describe the way in which I know this. It is a kind of intuitive knowledge. I believe that man is capable of knowing in many other ways than simply through the senses. There is an extra dimension of knowing, or extra-sensory perception as it is called today. How it works and what it is, no one knows, but it is there. With this mysterious capacity I know that Jesus is alive and that I can relate to him, and what is more, he relates to me. Prayer is not just a one-way process. This is something that cannot be explained or described to anyone who does not know it. But when I am relating to him he is relating to me. I know this is true. I may be deluding myself but I don't think I am. The reality of my relationship with Jesus Christ is all of a piece with my experience of reality in all other forms. I don't have to go into a trance when I pray. I do not need special surroundings (although they can help), and I am not being another kind of person than the person I am all the rest of the time. It is simply me relating to him and he to me.

In loneliness, aloneness and solitude, he is there. Standing with me in the first, helping me to go into the second, and being the centre and source of the bliss of the last.